What Can I Tell You?

Selected Poems of Roberto Carlos Garcia

FLOWERSONG
PRESS

FlowerSong Press

flowersongpress.com

ISBN: 978-1-953447-64-7

Library of Congress Control Number: 2022944842

Cover art: "Poppies" (oil paint on canvas) by Roberto Carlos Garcia

Cover design & layout: Ann Hagerty

Agitations both tender and muscular simmer inside these poems. A sadness that's palpable and physical haunts this poet; so does rage at the power-mongers' forces that keep children hungry, that fester poverty in terrifying mutations. Poet of engagement, Garcia speaks to the moon, to his sister, to the seasons and the garden, to his body a vessel: "these hands like a chunk of asteroid" full of taking & giving." This book offers us a photo-real blueprint of one man's life-space, an elegant blues-print of one man's heart, with direct utterance and lavish music.

—**Judith Vollmer**, author of *The Sound Boat: New & Selected Poems*.

Roberto Carlos Garcia is, it seems to me, poet-kin of both Lorca and Neruda, but also things like rain, wind, the color yellow and the color green. In Melancolía we have a collection of gorgeously quiet poems rendered by intellect and the dream where lyricism is born out of the dusky space between mystery and the everyday. Here is a breathtaking archive of an imagination at work, a body made up of effort and world. See: "My friends I am not above you // I can hear the song of reckoning in the rose thorns" and "In my mouth melancolÃa is an orchard, /a yellowing day & bluing night, // In my ribcage Melancolía is an ecstatic lilt /made of pearls, my heart wet sand, /pungent as dogwoods."

—**Aracelis Girmay**, author of *The Black Maria*.

In these sensuous poems everything is up for inspection and interrogation, including the speaker himself. Here are echoes of Lorca and Neruda, their depth and power, but in a voice entirely the poet's own. Roberto Carlos Garcia's poems take beauty as a gift, and also as a sometimes foil against capitalism and the numbness of the suburban life we are supposed to desire. "& what is poetry if not what we need?" We need poems like these, with their living language and their vision of where we are and where poetry, ecstatic and elegiac, can take us.

—**Anne Marie Macari**, author of *Red Deer*.

These poems ache and plead and yearn, and never forget song. Never forget song.

—**Ross Gay**, author of *Be Holding*.

Garcia's black / Maybe is the new standard for American race work in the 21st century. Through bouncy and superbly rich elegies, odes and essays, Garcia decimates notions of monolithic blackness and/or Dominican culture with language that haunts, hopes and howls. Every piece in this collection tugs at tomorrow while fueling itself with crumbs of yesterday. Masterful writing looks and sounds like black / Maybe.

    —**Kiese Laymon**, author of *Heavy*.

Roberto Carlos Garcia is, in his own words, an angry black man. Born of Castilian gypsies and Papa Africa, born of Trujillo's blood bath, the marked Dominican colonized, the worker's class, born American and city poor only to go incognito, a Suburban single-family latINO, he is a poet who refuses to lie or play nice, who refuses to be owned or named. black / Maybe is a brilliant mixed-self drama of historic proportions, complete with an intruding chorus of the wise and the dead. I hear a casting call to the culpable. I hear my own republic being sang.

    —**Rebecca Gayle Howell**, author of *American Purgatory*.

García openly confronts racism: ideological, institutional, interpersonal, internalized, and intersectional; he calls for a healing, for a seeing of blackness as beautiful in the sun. In black / Maybe, García invokes the dramatic chorus to offer commentary on the complexities of Afro-Latinx identity. Through voces afrodescendientes, García engages in an experiential, existential, and historical hermeneutics. We are invited into the familiar spaces in which we learn and question who we are, where we are prodded to redefine ourselves outside of an amorphous whiteness. García reveals the bricks within us, that hide who we are, behind which we have only ourselves to meet// ourselves to beat, // only ourselves/ to eat.

    —**Dr. Raina J. León**, author of *black god mother this body*.

The power and necessity of the poet resides in his/her or their willingness to mature with language alongside time's continuum—for the sake of the historical and humanity. What I mean is that Roberto Carlos Garcia's third collection, Elegies, is poetically structured through the lament of love, an elegiac love that he has come to recognize through temporal space, and how this examination manifests itself in the love of culture, the love of melanated skin, the love of family and the love of self. When Garcia makes the lyrical avowal: "I don't want to be afraid of love/I want to know where to love from," it is unmistakable that this poet has been searching for that calibrated center from which to create a dirge of observation, not only in the beautiful but also the undeniable ugly that terrorizes within the construction of race. Elegies is an exercise in the precision of craft, and I heart these poems for the aftersensation they create in the body: hope, empathy, and love.

—**Randall Horton**, author of *Dead Weight*.

When a poet is born into the world, they are met by a chaos for which they need forms to see. In Roberto Carlos Garcia's [Elegies], we must qualify that birth: When a Black poet is born into the world, they must quickly rock a coat of resistance, become attached to witness and fearless remembering, understand that poems can be shaped into weapons, bouquets, fire, and testimony. Roberto Carlos Garcia is that poet that cuts to the heart of the question: What is life? But, again, for this poet, the question has to be reexamined, restated, or remixed. In [Elegies], the question, beautifully answered, intrepidly addressed, becomes: What is life for a Black boy-cum-poet-cum-man in a world of unrelenting stares, judgement, and oppression? Fortunately, we have in Roberto Carlos Garcia a poet who has just enough fight to confront history and erasure with a daily naming of names, respect for this literary tradition and lineage, and an obligation to battle dominant tropes. He is in that class of necessary poets, our neighborhood's panacea against forgetting, and a primer on writing a book with just enough love to save us all.

—**Willie Perdomo**, author of *The Crazy Bunch*.

Roberto Garcia's singular voice is at its most potent in this remarkable book, which is grounded and glorified by a centerpiece of lyrically evocative elegies, both rough-hewn and tender, which lay bare the poet's longing and his unremitting quest to fill the gaping hollow left behind by the death of his revered grandmother. Although he writes "& the moon offers only the cold silver of struggle," there is also incessant muscle here—the birthing of the "mixtape," an addictive new poetic form; "A Tempest" a gorgeously inspired otherworld inhabited by Garcia's mother and father, and the book's solo prose offering, a bitter and blade-edged essay that seeks, yet again, to ascertain the utter urgency of the black life.

—**Patricia Smith**, author of *Incendiary Art*.

Table of Contents

Books by Roberto Carlos Garcia

Poetry

Melancolía

black /*Maybe: An Afro Lyric*

[Elegies]

Prose

Traveling Freely [essays]

for Kayana

Beautiful Rebellion, Affect, and Craft in Roberto Carlos Garcia's Poetry

The poems selected in Roberto Carlos Garcia's *What Can I Tell You?* command attention. The voice we hear in them exudes an ongoing affective rapport with the poet's implicit interlocutors. The very title of the volume suggests an interactive exchange. Dominant in that exchange is the speaker's unabashed avowal of emotion—no less than reason—as a means of engagement with the world. The speaking voice stands out for its urgency to feel and to care for, or to empathize with the social, botanical, and overall earthly milieu, expressing concern for or solidarity with the composite *ecology* within reach of the poet's heart. The radically sentient quality of the voice pervades nearly every poem in a way that never veers toward monotony, largely because of the expansiveness of the affective ground toward which the speaker trains his eyes. It could be an interpersonally fractious relation, as in these lines from "What Can I Tell You?", the poem from which the collection takes its title:

> From you I learned jilting
> doesn't require stepping away
>
> I confess
> I drink your furious glow
> like the color black,
> like a poet
>
> whose mouth is a bucket,
> whose head is an ocean of roses

In labeling this poem "*an ars poetica*" by way of epigraph, the poet provokes us to read in it a significant principle for his poetics.

The stark lyricism, rich imagery, and overall prosodic control evident in these lines also stress an area of concern that is salient in Garcia's selected poems, namely the poet's serious engagement with craft, poetic forms, literature in general, and creative expression within the arts and beyond. The poet converses with visual artists, musicians, and writers from literary and art history globally. Witness his gesture to the 1916 iconic painting *Melancholy of Departure* by the avantgarde Italian artist Giorgio de Chirico. The painting provides the poet with an apt metaphor to frame the state of mind that he ascribes to himself, his "melancolía," a disposition akin in his view to the notion of *duende* made current by Federico García Lorca, the notable Spanish poet of the 1927 Generation. Cultural references in *What Can I Tell You?* range from the Hebrew Bible, Christianity, Islamic rituals, Egyptian hieroglyphic symbols (*ankh*) of spiritual value, and a Yiddish term here (*tchotchke*) or an evocative Urdu word there (*goya*). The poet often salutes authors from across the ages either by using their words as epigraphs, by acknowledging an intertextual rapport between his work and theirs (—*after Rilke*), or borrowing lines from them to use as titles to his poems. A brief sampling of the literary figures thus invoked here would include the 13th century Persian poet Rumi, 19th century English Romantic poet Percy Bysshe Shelley, or 20th century authors such as Polish poet Czslaw Miloz, African American fiction writer and essayist James Baldwin, Syrian poet Adonis, African American poet Gwendolyn Brooks, Colombian novelist Gabriel García Márquez, and Turkish poet Nazim Hikmet, plus authors generationally closer to him.

Illustrative of the practice to put poetry in conversation with other arts is "*ars poetica*," a poem composed "after García Lorca" in which the speaker starts by putting his cards on the table:

> If nothing else it /
>   must be beautiful /
> Rebellion; /
> like Miles Davis' *Sketches of Spain*, /
>
> or pearl-topped street lamps /
> against green-brown trees

The poem's aesthetic injunction closes with the demand for "*Duende* / like shards of colored glass / shattered along a winding path, / catching bits of moonlight / in beautiful rebellion." Juxtaposing a revered Spanish poet with a great African American trumpeter and composer equalizes their value as seminal sources informing the artistic worldview that Garcia enacts in "*ars poetica.*" One gathers that the equalizing principle is the superior craft of both artists, and that such a principle encompasses not only literature, music, and fine arts, put also dance, the popular art forms stemming from hip-hop, expressive culture broadly, and ordinary creativity of the kind displayed by individuals who seem to blend an aesthetic sense into their everyday lives.

The *[Elegies]* section of the volume includes "Elegy in which is hidden an ode to your beehive updo," a piece that reminisces nostalgically about the speaker's maternal grandmother as he looks keenly at a "crinkly sepia photo" from the 1960s, around the time when she came to New York City from her native Dominican Republic. It is her eye for elegance that most strikes him—especially her hairstyle, which makes him wish she were around so they could go to the superstore to "laugh at the fake updos on sale," and in praise of her dexterity, he could tell her, "no one rocked it like you." It is the skillful artistry of grandma's hairdo that wins the day here.

Garcia's verse salutes superior skill even in the realm of sports, as we see in "Testament for the Crossover Dribble that Rocked the World," a 4-poem sequence in *[Elegies]* evoking a 12 March 1997 basketball game remembered for the dexterous performance of Allen Iverson of the Philadelphia 76ers. Iverson executed a crossover dribble so swift that the nearly invincible Michael Jordan of the Chicago Bulls could not see it. In evoking the thrill of athletic competition in the iconic American game, the poetic sequence inscribes itself in a long history of verse that captures the drama of contenders on the sports arena going back at least to the epics by the 8th century BCE Ionian bard Homer which abound in sports epithets.

Parallel to Garcia's exultation of skill and accomplished performance on the sports arena is a touching poem set against the backdrop of the song "Happy" by American rapper Pharrell Williams. The speaker listens to the song as he song as he exercises, "doing Couch to 10K." His fitness moves and the background music combine to trigger thoughts of his beloved grandma, "Mami." He travels back to joyful moments when they would dance, which they did routinely even after dementia deprived her of other abilities:

> …even Alzheimer's
> couldn't steal the words to your favorite bachatas
> or steal the muscle memory of your easy two step,
> & was I happy because I remember us dancing,
> was I happy because you never forgot how to dance
> was I happy because you never forgot how to sing
> or was I happy because in those ten fog filled years
> you were happy all the time & unaware of how we clapped
> along to any glimpse of the old you."

The poem's juxtaposition of rap lyrics and sounds with a tender memory of the poet's life with his dementia-stricken late grandmother accomplishes a stunningly effective crossing of aesthetic borders. It's hard to imagine a more humane outcome from the union of literature and rap than we get the verses of "Elegy in which 'Happy' by Pharrell sends me spiraling."

Garcia's devout exploration of poetic forms in his verse and his homage to the artistry of others, as well as his recognition of superior craft irrespective of the art form involved, operates as a continuum in these selected poems. He pays tribute to the ghazal, which started with the Arabs before going on to serve as a mainstay of medieval Persian bards, and to the ancient Japanese literary form called *zuihitsu* that allows writers to combine genres and registers as dictated by their mood with no regard for the structure of a predetermined outcome. Garcia gestures to the cento, a composition made by plucking lines from the verse of other poets. Linked etymologically to Greek and Roman roots and translated into English as "patchwork," the cento allows poets to cull varying materials from existing verse to produce meaning of their own. Conversing with the cento tradition, Garcia has put forward the "mixtape," a literary form of his own invention that he distinguishes from its antecedent in that, unlike the cento that limits its assemblage to lines plucked from other poets' verse, his "mixtape" casts a much larger net to borrow from prose fiction, "non-fiction, rap lyrics, & other forms of literature," as we read in one of his endnotes to the collection *[Elegies]*.

Garcia's "Author's Note" to his first poetry book muses about the causes of *melancolía*, the state of mind that he ascribes to himself, which colors the bulk of the volume:

> "What then causes melancolía in us? What brings on our symptoms? Is it the world's lack of social justice, is it racism, is it war, is it heartbreak, the death of loved ones, the fear of death, the accumulation of perceived slights and offenses, loneliness, unrequited love, unfulfilled desire, the fear of God, of heaven or hell, the lack of courage, poverty, the overwhelming ignorance pervading our world, the endless list of isms and phobias, the apocalypse, the death of a rose?"

This melancholic questioning and the artistic surrender that it demands deeply inform the content of *What Can I Tell You? Selected Poems of Roberto Carlos Garcia*, not only the texts coming from the poet's first book of poetry or from *[Elegies]*, his third, but also, and no less crucially, from **black**/*Maybe [An Afro Lyric]*. When addressing disturbing issues of white supremacy in the United Sates, negrophobic racism and anti-Haitian prejudice in Dominican society, the homeland of his ancestors, the obsession with Caucasian features among dark-skinned families with mixed ancestries, and social justice concerns overall, which form the kernel of **black**/*Maybe*, the speaker maintains the stance of the seeker of truth, "like a Sufi," an explorer of difficult realities. As the subject of **black**/*Maybe* is most overtly invested in race, racism, and phenotype, issues that trouble the poet most vexingly, it is no wonder that the texts from that book should display a degree of experimentation, diversity of registers, and formal shifts far greater than we find in *Melancolía* and *[Elegies]*.

In *What Can I Tell you? Selected Poems* Garcia puts to use his verbal dexterity and the expansive contours of his affective reach to find or intuit understanding of often insurmountable problems. An artist who dares to defy borders of knowledge and forms of utterance to make sense of the hurt prevailing in the world, he cares deeply for the composite ecology within reach of his heart, opening an enticing door for us to enter his compassionate realm and join his quest for understanding.

Dr. Silvio Torres-Saillant
Syracuse University
May 17th, 2022

Introduction

What Can I Tell You? Selected Poems of Roberto Carlos Garcia brings together the best works from this poet's previously published collections. This volume offers new readers a powerful entry into García's oeuvre and decidedly establishes his place within Dominican American, Caribbean, AfroLatinx, and Black Diasporic letters. Poems from *Melancolía,* **black***/Maybe: An Afro Lyric,* and *[Elegies],* trace an oppositional poetics marked by loss and grief, ranging from the deeply personal to the global and political. Above all, we witness the power of vulnerability, evident when the poet intimates "This book [*Melancolía*] is a product of my sacred struggle with melancolía." This level of vulnerability is refreshing considering the strict gender norms that predominate in Latin American and Latinx societies, and the stigma that persists around mental health issues. In the midst of the struggle, including mourning his younger sister's death, the speaker turns to poetry as an instrument of healing.

There is also a palpable sense of loss in the speaker's awareness of how race and class have rendered him invisible: "I am unseen—I am conjured," he tells us. Blackness, however, takes more of a center stage in the selected poems from his second poetry collection, **black***/Maybe: An Afro Lyric.* In these works, grief remains a constant. How could it not, given the symbolic, verbal, and physical violence that the speaker experiences and witnesses around him because of racism?

However, García acknowledges pain but does not dwell on it, and this acceptance drives him to question, challenge, and confront colonialism's legacy of anti-Blackness. As an AfroLatinx, the speaker finds himself having to defend his *negritud* vis-a-vis both African Americans and Dominicans. Affirming his Blackness becomes simultaneously an outward- (U.S. society) and inward-directed (Dominican culture/family) gesture. Feeling slighted by a Black poet in the poem "The day a poet I looked-up-to *clowned* me," the speaker reflects:

Oh, you're not Black black?
& I'm cast off
aboard my great-great
grand-pappy's Middle-Passage,
his slaver to
the blue-skied,
salt sea air of Caribbean cane-fields
Same all-inclusive package
as our cousins in Virginia

Through these verses, the speaker asserts his Blackness, reminding the reader that his African ancestors also survived the Middle Passage. The last two verses challenge U.S.-centered understandings of slavery and Blackness. By drawing familial links between the enslaved Africans who were forcibly taken to what is now the United States and those who were brought to Latin America and the Caribbean, the poem affirms transhemispheric Blackness and its shared history. The dialogue that Garcia's poetry establishes with figures such as James Baldwin, Aimé Césaire, Amiri Baraka, Willie Perdomo, and Miguel Piñero, among others, grounds his works within a robust transhemispheric Black genealogy.

The defense of Blackness also extends to the more intimate terrain of family and community. We hear the matriarchal archetype, Mamá Ana, telling the speaker "No somos negros," a phrase that registers the anti-Blackness that prevails among many sectors of Dominican and Latinx society. Elaborating on this point in his essay "black *Maybe*," García states: "I'm black in a country that by all indications hates black people, and I'm descended from people that are black, but pretend not to be black." With this statement, the author decries the different layers of racism that he experiences as a Dominican and an AfroLatino in the United States. He also denounces both U.S. and Dominican/Latinx white supremacy, the latter a legacy of the *casta* system imposed by Spanish colonialism. Tracing the connections between colonial history, U.S. Empire, the anti-Haitianism and anti-Blackness that were codified during Rafael Trujillo's bloody thirty-year regime, and La Sentencia—the 2013 law that denationalized over one hundred thousand Dominicans of Haitian descent—the essay addresses head on some of the central racial taboos of Dominican society.

Loss and grief are also central in García's selected poems from *[Elegies]*, his third poetry collection. Most of the poems, as the title indicates, are elegies, including to his deceased father and maternal grandmother (Mami), who raised him and suffered from Alzheimer's disease, an illness that is quite prevalent among people of color, especially in Black and Latinx communities.[1] The verse "I realize that to remember is to grieve" encapsulates the heart of the speaker's struggle in these poems. The works in this section are intimate and deeply personal, and like previous works, do not shy away from confronting pain. But this pain goes beyond the personal. The poem "Elegy for all of it" offers a reflection on the impact of symbolic and physical anti-Black violence. The verses "The Monday after Tamir Rice's murder / many white people I knew went on with their lives" decry the disconnect between those whose lives are protected by white privilege and those who—like the AfroLatino speaker—don't have a choice but to live in fear of violence due to the color of their skin. The last section of the poem lists the names of about fifty, mostly Black (and some Black Latinx), murder victims, especially at the hands of the police:

> "Eric Garner Michael Brown Tamir Rice
> Walter Scott Alton Sterling Philando Castile
> Stephon Clark Breonna Taylor George Floyd"

The poem ends with the verse "Every year, of every decade, there is a list. Remember that," demanding that as readers we see not just the humanity of all Black people, but that we recognize the systemic racism that perpetuates the violence in order to stop it.

What Can I Tell You? Selected Poems of Roberto Carlos Garcia offers readers a beautifully curated selection of Garcia's previously published works. For the uninitiated reader, this powerful and thought-provoking volume offers an entry into the poetic oeuvre of someone who I consider to be one of the most important AfroLatinx poets of his generation. His poetry is proof that, as the poetic voice affirms (in the quote from Gwendolyn Brooks), "Our world survives / on two things: first the poet & second the poet."

Dr. Marisel Moreno
University of Notre Dame
March 8, 2022

---

[1] The National Institute on Aging has stated that "Overall, 13 percent of U.S. Latinos aged 65 and older are thought to have Alzheimer's or a related dementia, lower than for African Americans and higher than for non-Hispanic whites, the CDC estimates." According to the Alzheimer's Association, "Among Black Americans ages 70 and older, 21.3% are living with Alzheimer's".

I am interested in telling my particular truth as I have seen it.

—Gwendolyn Brooks

We make a living out of the things a system prohibits, refuses, denigrates, and throws away. We study everything.

—Patrick Rosal

I imagine a poet
into whose innards history pours
drenching his words and pooling at his feet,
a poet who rains blood that some hoist as a banner made of sky.

—Adonis

Melancolía

On *Melancolía*

Melancolía is as easily defined as its elusive cousin, *Duende*. Which is another way of saying it is indefinable. Ancient and medieval physicians believed an excess of one or more of the four primary bodily fluids caused it. I won't bore you with that. You can Google it or visit a library. I'm more interested in what it does to poets. In the way melancolía makes poets long for things that have been, that have yet to pass, and that might have never existed. It makes a poet ache for the beauty and the brevity of life—the fleeting scent and brightness of the rose's many dresses, of spring and summer's shifting heat, and for the childhood that could have been. Melancolía is thirst for joy and believe it or not, pain. It is the heat of lust and the shame of lusting, of not being able to have the thing or person you desire. Melancolía is pure longing and the restless, depressed, and wretched anxiety of longing. And yet it is significantly more complicated than that. We experience melancolía physically.

In her essay collection *Sidewalks*, Valeria Luiselli describes the symptoms of melancolía as "sadness, crying, stress, headaches, chest pains, insomnia, fatigue, and hallucinations." I'd also add a peculiar unquenchable thirst for wine. These pains must be expressed, poured out, painted, sung, or written. The struggle must be given life. Here is where the evil little cousin *Duende* knocks incessantly at our door. Melancolía feeds the monster—it feeds Duende. Garcia Lorca wrote, "We only know that he [*duende*] burns the blood like a poultice of broken glass, that he exhausts, that he rejects all the sweet geometry we have learned, that he smashes styles, that he leans on human pain with no consolation…" He also wrote that an old maestro of the guitar told him, "The *duende*, then, is a power, not a work. It is a struggle, not a thought." I take "thought" to mean overthinking, the draining of life from the artistic idea, leaving the body and retiring completely into the mind. Trying to shake off melancolía, to shake off the pain or experience that feeds the art.

What then causes melancolía in us? What brings on our symptoms? Is it the world's lack of social justice, is it racism, is it war, is it heartbreak, the death of loved ones, the fear of death, the accumulation of perceived slights and offenses, loneliness, unrequited love, unfulfilled desire, the fear of God, of heaven or hell, the lack of courage, poverty, the overwhelming ignorance pervading our world, the endless list of isms and phobias, the apocalypse, the death of a rose? How then to express this, to be a poet that masters melancolía and the mysterious and dangerous outburst of expression that is *duende*? I don't pretend to know, but I give in to it. I simply enjoy the struggle, the fight to understand. Not thought but contemplation, like a Sufi seeking truth.

This book is a product of my sacred struggle with melancolía.

No currency

My loveseat in suburbia is distance
between me & the world beyond the flat screen,
a world I'd love to crush like a dictator,
a sad dictator,

El Generalissimo Ridiculissimo,
for this world where children burn

like the dry bush of California countryside,
where firefighters come to save the houses, & die

From my loveseat in suburbia
as useful as a clown's nose—

After all, who can afford water?

I'm a father of three, growing fat Meanwhile
hunger is killing nations / gluttony is killing nations,
I wear floppy feet

but as *El Generalissimo,* I will complete the carnage,
the crazy complicity

Ah, poets!

We are one & the same—rabble what you rabble

Divine a poem,
or a poet, for that matter

What you imply is fireworks,
but the truth is empty wine bottles

Water is made clear by the current,
if it be hell say it is hell

From my loveseat in suburbia, I do nothing,
but *El Generalissimo* can instigate metamorphosis

Kids, what should we turn into / what will become of us?
Pass me the remote control

Melancolia

—after Giorgio De Chirico's Melancholia, 1916

At times I feel broad like shadows in a courtyard,
or insignificant, a faraway speck squinting from the moon,

I am obsessed,
but without an object

Husband, father, son—
but in the sun I cry easily
like a child lamenting a fallen ice cream cone,
the fine line between caring & catatonia
dust in a sun ray

I self-medicate—wine
until the questions become clear

I suppose the symmetry of fresh-cut lawns,
polished cars, & opposing driveways
is the only dunce cap I can wear,
my flag in the wind & I don't believe in it

A nun, Sister Elizabeth, taught me a song:
she says she's holding out hope for me:

This is the day the Lord has made
Let us rejoice and enjoy it

It's in my head as I count the tchotchkes
listen to trains in the distance,
& wander from light to dark
between the rooms in my house

Whispers

The wind outside my window is doubt:
it reminds me that words are insufficient,

that we can only remake the past as lies,
so I promise never to dream in pencil again;
I will paint red, blue, & green oil memories,

letters textured like toothpaste

I will prick all ten fingertips & paint in blood,
even if the words
don't promise to last any longer

How do the evergreens in my yard stand immortality,
the wind coaxing their needles to fall?

I warn my kids: *Be careful. They're pointy. You'll bleed:*
who'll keep me tethered here?

Words, pencils, oils, & blood—
I'm carrying on
All things dance their way to dust,
but I must stay here

Let's refuse
Come leap through the keyhole with me:
don't open the door

Behind my window dreams are better without permission:
there's no wind to wipe the canvas white again

This is not an elegy

This is not an elegy, but I was haunted,
mesmerized by how ablaze leaves are in death,
the yellow red browns scattered across my lawn
& I felt my little sister sitting there
she's been gone six years now—
felt her caress like autumn winds
the kind that don't go back empty-handed,
& I believed in spring resurrection,
but the leaves cried like poppy fields
& she floated away

Autumn's ruse, the artifice
of leaves falling from trees—
I can't name it

Heal thy self

There's some ancient wisdom in paper cuts,
in allegedly harmless things & carelessness,

that we are naked as glass is naked,
blind like sunlight in what we burn,
pebbles hurled callously shattering worlds

I watch a few bumblebees stick their long hairy tongues
deep into the heads of blooming rose beds

How delicious to drink & be sated by such beauty,
to forget what ties me to the animal world,
mortgages, & hard swallows

Let's name each other according to our birthmarks

I want to live like the nectar from a rose—
warm river inside the withering reds & yellows—
to live like nectar carried off by the bumblebees,
a little spilled here, a little pissed there

Moon dreams
—after Miles Davis

I hear the crag sound
of trash dragged
down cold ashen asphalt

I check the lock on the door,
go to the kitchen window
where moonlight's bath softens
a praying wind's *Diana, Diana,*

& the whole yard's bright as daytime
The trees, grass, & houses
under a chrome bulb

Moon, every many-legged thing
from my nightmares praises you tonight,

a raucous pagan feast
of strangeness in the shadows

Sleepless moon–silver night,
only dawn quiets the exhausted revelry

Moon, drunk in a burning sky,

shining out of agony,
reigning over a bit of time,

& foolish lovers moan
in moonlight dripping
through midnight's blinds

We are drawn to the moon
like animals baffled
at their own reflections

The hunter's moon,
an overripe grapefruit sticky
& oozing a luminous liquor

I kneel open-mouthed swallowing
air but the moon refuses to fall;

it goads me, a bending branch
pretending to break
as my tongue & throat beg & pray

& the sea inside me
riots for release

Full moon lullaby,
Diana, Diana

I walk with her under an April moon:
she doesn't speak;

my tongue trembles
at the sight of the nearing woods
& the scent of spring lovemaking in the night

She smiles and smiles

I follow

Duplicity

Hard truth:

First thing I do
as I breathe into a room
is search
for brown & black faces,
bobbing in America's
post racial waters

I swim peripheral glances
Back-stroke being ignored
Wade on a chair
in a corner of the room
& chat up the Help

until,

some (not brown or black) one
tosses me
an integration life-
line

Hard truth:

Light & Dark
sparkle the waters
like tinsel,
pretty chimera

No one really
has to

Does anyone *really*
have to?

Talk to me—

Savior complex

1.

Kneel & make salt five times a day

If the world knew what birds know of love—
each one of you could be part of me

Think how many could be saved
I too am able to watch the world burn
from a deck in the woods, a drink in my hand

We believe that's okay

2.

Supplicate the Father, the Son & the Holy Spirit

I agree about wine, bread, & olives—vespers
I'll hold hands with you,
& we'll listen to one another's pain

The love between us a peace accord,
an oasis in hell, a dream temple
we enter asleep, only

3.

Say ten Hail Marys—look around—repeat

On my knees I pretend to be a tsunami
washing away the suffering—
resurrecting the damned from the sea as clouds

My hands in adulation: *Up there*, I say *Look up there!*
The meek shall inherit fresh ink,
& Earth shall inherit a new story

You & I must continue to pray

4.

Give zakat to the poor & needy

I can no longer make a fist—neither to hit nor to hide things
I hear fire redeems best
My friends, I am not above you—

I can hear the song of reckoning in the rose thorns

This body

My world dangles
on a wisp of spider web,

knees ache & knuckles pop,

& wet or hard,
hunger is a bicep flexing,
a madness for heat & touch
so natural its breath is dirt

Pray God breaks the fever,
run an ice cube from your breast
to your navel,

drip the cold on your sex,
for all the good it will do you

The poem you asked for
for Yesenia Montilla

I watched a white heron alight on a lake
& turned the image into another,
of my soul departing from heaven
as a mustard seed on a river of blood

I don't know why I go there,
my body—lost in the wild hunger of skin,
free from an ether I can no longer feel—
groping breathing suffering

I ache for sensation,
for cold nights under starlight
& hot showers

Perhaps a truth about me will rise
from the crusted muddy surface of this poem

I care what you think of it,
but within measure;
you asked for a poem—now here I am
naked & throbbing on the page

Self-medicate

I'm keeping the moon in a mason jar with wine;
when it shines at a right angle I swig
openmouthed, belch sparks, nuzzle deeper
into the soil's shoulder, into a bed of dead leaves,
& pray it all catches fire

Then I'll be an ember on a blazing landscape—
I'll be like the stars

Self-portrait in American black
(for the silent)

I am that I am—what America TV's me;
       monstrous chameleon,
       schizophrenic Janus,

transformed, transmuted—
       switching black image
       for your mind's white eye / I

I line up the game winner:
       Shoot it!
       I stand arms raised

I am on the corner:
       Don't shoot!
       I stand arms raised

the crowd gives a standing ovation

I stand mic in hand, arms raised:
       I am a god, now hurry up wit my damn massage!
       the crowd sings along

I am unseen—I am conjured:
       I am that I am the entertainment
       you seek when you need
       to dance
       to sport
       to laugh
       to cry
       to feel like God

I am that I am what
  America's narrative makes me:
  A STRUGGLE ENSUES,
  A BRIEF ALTERCATION,
  & I stand as death's bride

arms raised—arms wide,
black play-doh
for your mind's white eye / I

Keeping on

—an American sonnet, after Gerald Stern

Morning cold is worst, rising from the ground
& grabbing at old ankle & knee injuries;
the new day opens like a horrific crash
I can't look away from, & the hope
that there are survivors becomes the thing
dragging me to the shower & hot water;
the steam makes me think of coffee,
dark & deep like the sleep I long to return to;
I step out to the second cold, dry off slowly;
life's conveyor belt accelerates; now it's about
keeping up, as the little voice grows louder
& louder until I'm sitting in the car, weighing
all the options, the infinite variations of doubt,
& what scares me most is not sitting still
but careening through space & time decaying
as quickly as the paths I choose not to travel,
& the voice grows louder, familiar from yesterday
& the day before, going so far back there's no point
looking—I listen as the voice becomes a song,
obey it, close my eyes, & give thanks

Melancolía

> *Walk into my cage and ask the lions*
> —Frank Lima

In my mouth melancolía is an orchard,
a yellowing day & bluing night

In my ribcage melancolía is an ecstatic lilt
made of pearls, my heart—wet sand,
pungent as dogwoods

In the graveyard of my head,
in the lion's mouth salty & wet,

in the endless paso doble
of my lungs—melancolía

In the absence, the nothingness,
the lean parched tongue of longing,
in the winding along a cobble stone path

in this desolate garden,
in my voice unheard, choked by dirt,
in the secret of dew
& scent of rebirth downwind
melancolía

In weeping sorrowful or joyful tears,
in lying here among the animals,

on my knees in my fear of God,
through my doubts in fatherhood,
in feasting & drinking, in starving,
during nightmares & dreams,
in passion & apathy,
in life & death & in between—

melancolía

What can I tell you?

—an ars poetica

I confess
from you I learned
sweat is poison as well as nectar,

& there is no good word
for how I linger as you exhale

I confess
I am a cracked mirror,
& you are a stone, a bird,
starlight tickling the fractures

From you I learned jilting
doesn't require stepping away

I confess
I drink your furious glow
like the color black,
like a poet

whose mouth is a bucket,
whose head is an ocean of roses

"You just have to play it by ear, and pray for rain"
—*James Baldwin*

My guardian angel is tired,
the crick in her neck a pinched nerve
that makes her fingers numb;

she's ready for bright velour jumpsuits
& Crocs

I push life I push it like I know I'm protected

My friend called me,
dreamed he was at my funeral

Happens all the time, I said:
I'm not peeking around corners,

jerking my head to the cardinal points
I wonder about replacements though;

perhaps I'll write a love poem
& woo a new guardian angel

I feel like I ate too much cornbread
& forgot to ask for a drink

Hear my prayer, Lord:
this life is a mirror in a lightning storm,
a trumpet solo on a splintered stage,

a footrace against a faster man,
a child picking daffodils

Before I start my prayer, tell me,
are angels really androgynous?

Drive

I'm listening to Vampire Weekend
on my drive home, & I wouldn't know
what a Vampire Weekend is except
that my daughter made me a playlist
for my fortieth birthday; & I'm grateful
we listen to so much music together,
because I can't stop dancing to this track,
track three, & I'm maybe speeding a little
thinking of how fast the years pass & come
up on you at the same time; & then I see
the biggest blackest raven you'd ever want
to see, pecking the red pulpy roadkill
of some poor beast too slow to swim life's
wave & there's nothing left but the strips
of its insides, & the raven's having its fill,
& isn't that the mystery? & if life isn't a road
you speed down, looking periodically
in the rearview as the houses, trees, people
& places whiz by, & if life isn't eating your
red pulpy guts at the same time as you eat
life's indigestible flesh, dancing, singing even
to a song full of sentiment, then we're doing it
wrong, I'm doing it wrong, & please tell me
what is more real than the peck-peck-peck
of devouring this life

Blood cake

poems with no lilies or moons / and no love affairs about to fail
—Federico García Lorca

The earth is a blood cake

Blood bubbling in the soil, in the sea,
dripping from the skies

Blood stretching in the wheat, the corn;
blood crackling in the rice fields

The colors on my palette,
red, yellow, black, brown, white—
herein is the world,

& yet blood means a man, a woman, a child

No crust, magma, or core,
only blood crying out
from the subconscious
of every living thing

Mother Earth will come calling

In the lakes, rivers, & oceans of blood,
in the fields, hills, & mountains of blood,
each rose, sunrise, & sunset;
blood limp in a champagne glass,

a toast to

        the tin taste

                of blood

                        in the cake

The apocalypse up close

1.

I tremble in a strange column

I hold a weapon (a sword, a gun, a bomb, poison,
words,) & the rest of this regiment—

brothers, daughters, grandmothers, & sick people—
all carry the weapon; black, white, gay,

straight, yellow, red, we number in the millions—
At the head of each column a captain

reads from the Bible, the Koran, the Talmud, a book of poems
& froths at the mouth for theater

There is doom in the air, thirst at the back of our throats;
in our mouths we know we must kill—

we are scared, weeping aimless tears;
we name our weapons: *Apathy, Dissatisfaction*

Banners convulse in a half wind, & we stand
on a beach of salt & iron,

to our right a rock wall, to our left the sea full of orcas,
across from us another army

full of people I know & a cry rising,
the petty grievances of the apocalypse:

He denied me a plate of food:
She wouldn't sleep with me:
He never listened to my advice:
She was more successful—
More beautiful,
He broke my heart:
He's not a believer—

Never took me seriously:
An ass kisser:
She's a racist:
He's an Uncle Tom:
She never calls me back:

Only the bugle, loud as a skyscraper
crumbling calls us to action

We charge, the weapon firing
slight & deliberate pain—

I recognize my loved ones,
& they recognize me,

but we tear flesh from limb anyway,

& with each death the sea is roiling, a flood
of blood & guilt hardening sand to cement, the killing

so difficult many die while killing,
hearts give out, aneurisms burst

We're butchers—bloody gut water up to our chins,
until we drown choking on each other

2.

No taking five, people
How did it apocalypse?
We lived the long way around,

reneged mercy & sympathy,
defaulted the world flat again,
disproved everything

Time now for reckoning;
no slogans, jingles, or yellowing
the cosmos happy-as-fuck-it

We plead not guilty, apocalypse—
we redeem our acts;
the world was our stage, not our fault

We reject adjudication (while rubbing
at the dry blood on our skin,) but it clings
like the will to live, or some smell,

& the executioner walks in
humming a tune, turns to us:
If you can wash off the blood, you're forgiven
He buckets water on us:
the more we wash, the bloodier
we get, red then oily black,

& we drown in blood again,
another death, a darker night,
being crushed in the mouth of an orca

We scream we will come out clean
on the other side; we hear
the executioner shout, *No chance*

3.

We repent! We repent;
it's dark down here We
repent; we can't see or smell
We repent! We repent;

our form is formless We
repent; we can't believe this We
want a cold one, a smoke!
We repent! For God's sake,

isn't that what we're supposed to say?

In white silence

America remains a matchstick;
a bundle of dry-wood—kerosene

I POST a STATUS,
you LIKE & COMMENT, but

we're just mouthing;
a script unfolds, a TV special,

& all the while black bodies—dandelions
breaking in quiet breezes

Our black bodies—dust peeling
off America's skin—

swept from a street corner,
a Wal-Mart, a park—our black bodies

dumped in Object, Other, Thing

A cold autumn day of white silence
of one minute a friend & the next   a space

a loyalty strange as strange fruit,
a privilege like air through teeth

White sister, brother,
I cannot make you feel

I paint the portrait
I danse macabre

I disintegrate in front of you, but
in white silence—there aren't even shadows

A riot in images

A hooded sweatshirt
hung upside down,
flag at half-mast

A cop huffs & puffs a teen down a city street:
one's running scared, one's running fast;

two hearts buck, one heart blown away
like a sandcastle in a storm

Weary eyes weep, observe
a void in a torso & another   *another*

Wooly black hair bloody
sponge matts the pavement

A dragon tail of white black & brown faces,
a cop searing like a conifer tree
in centuries-old-fire

Ash falls on lips & tongues, ash on eyelids—
heaps of ash from the reckoning;

bricks melt like butter in the sun;
people melt like ice in rum

Mercy   Mercy   Mercy
water on cracked bleeding lips

Anchorite

Mornings I read the dew drops on my windshield
like an old *santero* divining
from a coffee cup & still I speak
my prayers into the world's mouth

because

"I gave Emily Dickinson to you then"
—Agha Shahid Ali

as if she were a cold or
a lasting heirloom,
a piece of my living soul

So dangerous to make woman metaphor
though I prefer to call her sea, ocean
All the mountains & hills removed

Emily,
is there room at your small wooden desk
for the waters & me?

I will hold your dress one-handed in the wind:
we'll take turns writing slant rhymes,
our feet gritty with sea salt,

my tongue a barn swallow
full of slang,
your eyes foam, black waves

I gave you, Emily,
to keep you;
this is how I love,

so I can rise
from your desk, your ocean,
soaked in lady slipper orchids

Belief system

I believe in the magic of kissing,
of low-cut dresses, too much wine,
& slow dancing

I believe you will be remembered
by how you make love,
& that loving is the best way
to know one another

I believe water was turned
into wine; it makes sense;
I wish I could've been there

I believe we are all mustard seeds,
yellow as stars & just as perilous
I believe we should rename ourselves—

I believe I love to the point of being
an imbecile,
then shrink like tissue

When I weep like this everyone hates me

Reading Rorschach cards

Fine white dust on a loaf of bread
Broken heart pounding in a lunch pail
Crooked crumbling concrete steps
Sunshine rolling 'round a wind-filled sail
Mother mending socks & underpants
Trees creaking in a moonlit wind
Rolled up trousers—winemaker's dance
Pins & needles, needles & pins
Leather shoes, leather belt, leather jacket
Crimson, ocher, cobalt, & umber fingernails
The night makes the aura, & the J can't hack it
Silver trail along a lane of slimy snails

A giant box of painted wooden toys
Birthday boy, birthday boy, birthday boy

Traffic

This poem takes place in traffic,
the traffic of bills at a set time every month,
of people, obstacles, & the self-inflicted

I went to pick up my little adjunct check,
wove through the traffic of red tape & slack

On my way home I sat in traffic
Stuck under the overpass I saw a pack of men
on the sidewalk blocking people traffic,

back & forth around a cardboard box,
like mall traffic, circulating
A man rose from the box & another took his place

I checked the clock; could I beat traffic to the bank
Everyone's rubbernecking, we see knees & feet,
hiked above the cardboard box & a man squatting,

& then last week's memory of a woman sulking,
          (in the same chair)
looking / scanning & now she's on the ground,
under a man who'll stand & walk off into traffic

A father crossed the street with his daughter
to circumvent the traffic made up of clots blocking

us up or laying us down in the guts of a box;
the traffic of set bills at a set time every month

or the rumble of a lack of traffic in our guts,
or the traffic of the next fix,
or just because there's too much traffic
& we want out

There is my mountain

There is my mountain,
a slim volume of poems
facedown in a rain puddle

I have no coat, no scarf,
& a beggar making fire says to me,
Bring the book—let's burn it

& what is poetry if not what we need?

Clean

The leaf blower does its work with ease,
& I'm reminded of dead skin or dust
in the corners of the house & how
our human bodies resemble the universe,
the heart like an engine, a star spreading
blood through a galaxy of flesh
I dig a hole with my hands pretending
to make a woman from the fresh
topsoil, the cilantro, & tomatoes,
these hands like a hunk of asteroid—
full of taking & giving, of friend & foe
kneeling in stubborn grass—like a little boy

I know the universe is within this body
& that somewhere along the way I forgot it

This is an elegy
—for Kyana

I thought I saw your face in the water,
so I followed flickering starlight down the pier,
jumping over the missing boards, wanting to go farther
The bartender called to me, *Okay out there?*
& I lost you in the white foam crashing below
On the sand I decided to roll up my pants & try again
The moon was steady then, & the sea wasn't cold,
just warm the way love is warm—I heard you calling
The bartender touched my back—*The sea,* he warned,
is the road between this world & the next—
he offered me a drink—*I've seen many handsome men called*

by the other side He had the bottle in his pocket
We sat down & got drunk in the water

Toil

My head against yours & I'm falling asleep;
the smell of your shampoo does that,
but I can't stop thinking about the lawn
& why I can't make grass grow on the dead parts;
my heart palpitates, signs of stress, no wine
tonight—too sleepy; & today was hot
& full of work in the yellow heat of a gift
of a day to remind us that yes, summer is real,
& then I look for a metaphor,
some device to explain my tiredness in the face
of such a happy event as an eighty-degree day,
perhaps raking the dead soil or sweeping
the neighbor's cigarette butts
or avoiding eye contact with *that* neighbor—
the one who called my yard ghetto, anonymously,
in a letter left in my mailbox, & then I realize
I miss the hood, the ghetto, the block, whatever;
sure, it was work, life & death work, but true,
what-life-is-about true—survival; & what this
has to do with the parched state of my lawn
I'm afraid to admit because it's too easy to work
hard against something while telling yourself
you're working to achieve it; & honestly
I sleep pretty good at night, but my toil,
so far as the green grass of neatly manicured
lawns, has been for naught; & that shit, my love,
along with wanting the neatly manicured lawn
& the "friendly" approval of neighbors,
contains the mystery that haunts me

"A poet is a nightingale who sits in darkness and sings"
—Percy Bysshe Shelley

I smell the rain before it rains,
my bones make excellent ears,
& simply my friends,
time has given me grizzle

I hear melancolía calling—
a long-distance relative
I'd rather ignore, but still
I'm curious to know if she sleeps
naked or not

I see I've lived in a rush,
making every endeavor a quickie
I am a drop of water falling
from a cloud made of too little time

Oh God, oh mysterious in the air God,
in that moment before I dream,
before I cum,
before I say, "I am resigned,"
before I put pencil to paper,

I imagine myself in the void
It is dark—a lover's nape—
familiar, yet foreign—always new
It is there that I wait for answers

ars poetica
　　　　—*after García Lorca*

If nothing else it
　　　　must be beautiful

Rebellion;
like Miles Davis' *Sketches of Spain*,

or pearl-topped street lamps
against green-brown trees,
green-blue grass against satin
mists of autumn sky so gray

birds flitting through
　　　　it make silent black & white movies,

or Thursday half-moon sighing,

　　　　against two feet floating free,
no boundaries; *Duende*

like shards of colored glass
shattered along a winding path,

catching bits of moonlight
　　　　in beautiful rebellion

black/*Maybe: An Afro Lyric*

It can be said that while there are differences in processes of racialization throughout the African Diaspora, in terms of categories that are used to define people, there are similarities when we consider slavery and racialist thinking…This positionality links people of African descent historically and contemporaneously, mapping a shared historical experience of slavery, systems of inequality, and relationships where racialized identity were created and recreated.

—Kimberly Eison Simmons, "Navigating the Racial Terrain: Blackness and Mixedness in the United States and the Dominican Republic"

…the awareness of being black, the simple acknowledgment of a fact which implies the acceptance of it, a taking charge of one's destiny as a black man [person], of one's history and culture…

—Aimé Césaire on *Négritude*

Chorus

Mamá Ana:

Mijo, por favor!

How many times can I say it?

     No somos negros,

we are tan! *Tu no eres Negro* (Throws her hands up)

     James Baldwin: To be Negro in *this* country

     and to be relatively conscious

     is

     to be in a rage

     almost   all the time

Mamá Ana's flat nose

Mamá,
if we *are* part Spanish gypsy,
            part Taino Indian,

why is your nose flat
like Celia Cruz?

Why's your hair deep waves
like Caribbean Sea,
skin never-before-seen cinnamon?
Why do I look like black Chinaman?

> *Mamá Pastora was Castilian gypsy, hair yellow*
> *Like piss from a rum hangover,*
> *Eyes blue like gunpowder flashing, skin white*
> *Like bones in the grave*
>
> *Papa Africa—Jose Maria, had hair tight*
> *As hide stretched over a drum,*
> *Lips full like the bellies of slave ships, skin Black*
> *Like bones in the grave*
>
> *My flat nose comes from deep inside them,*
> *Our skin, nose & hair an antenna*
> *To both ancestors,*
> *Beyond the grave*

We're not black, we're tan   Now callate!

Back to school

Plantains melted
onions & cheese
into the small sea of olive oil & salt
on my plate & after the meal,
after the glass of cold tamarind juice,
a nap in the shade, the smell
of palm soaked air,
sweet river water baptisms
I dreamt of Brenda Vazquez
& her Castilian slants,
Jessica Alba skin,
her already beautiful body in the fifth grade,
& I dreamt of going back to school,
sharing Dominican slang with her,
Popola, Aficiao, Coñaso—
I didn't want to vacation there at first
Mamá Ana warned me:
AVOID THE SUN. YOU ARE TOO BLACK ALREADY
But the sun taught me I belonged,
it loved me blacker, stronger
I went back to school
& sought Brenda Vazquez,
walked up to her & she said:
Hay que Negro, tu pareces un puro Negro!
& my friends on the playground froze
then laughed & repeated:
El Negro, el Negro, el Negro!
Damn, why did I feel so bad,
why have I been sitting barefoot
on this small patch of schoolyard grass
ever since?

Back to school (the B-side)

You ain't Black. You Spanish.
You Goya bean eatin'
Porteereecan

>   *I ain't Puerto Rican*

You ain't Black. You
think you Black but you ain't,
you Spanish

>   *I guess you English*

Whatchusay? Crazy Spanish boy,
you dark, a little bit
See me? Black

>   *Mm-hmm, you English too*

I know nothin' 'bout no England

>   *My grandpappy's massa was from Spain*
>   *Your grandpappy's massa was from England*
>   *So who Spanish?*
>   *Who English?*

A sense that something's happened

Then white snow began to fall
White snow so alluring, so ordered,

dressed trees in the less mundane,
made the paths mysterious

like life lines on a palm
Then someone keyed my car:

Fuck you in white against the navy blue,
keyed *Fuck you*—hid it in white snow,

we were surprised
Most of the white poets, like snow,

had floated into town together,
just them together, like high school,

like undergrad, like work,
the rest of us withdrew to the dorms,

drank wine, danced, a woman kissed me kindness,
I, grateful, tried to forget hate, we all wondered what to think

My professor asked me: *Do you think your car was keyed
because you're black?* I couldn't know for sure

We sensed something had happened
White snow returned—unyielding

Identity repair poem

NÉGRO

Négrito lindo (pretty)
Négrito chulo (smooth)
Querido négro (beloved)
Maldito négro (damn!)

SUGARCANE

Yeah, we go back
like sun & sweat
crack of the whip
greed & pain,
a trip across a cold salty ocean

AFRO-LATINO

Pedro Martinez
Jheri curls
Mongo Santamaria
Drums Drums Drums
Rum   Rum   Rum

LATINO (BLACK HISPANIC) CHECK HERE

LATINO (WHITE HISPANIC) CHECK HERE

I mean *soy negro*,
not Af-Am,
but I'm black
Verdad?

Mamá Ana's funny money

Mamá Ana said take
these purple, blue & green
pieces of New Deal bones
& go buy milk

I walked down the street clenching—
purple money?
Hidden in my fist
so no one could see

Crossing the street I almost got crushed
flat by a yellow cab but an old man
snatched me up
saved me
chastised me

You be careful, we don't accept
food stamps here!
You coulda been killed!
Watch where you crossin'!
Don't you know?
We don't accept food stamps here!

I ran to the store, saw
my neighbor leaving, she said:
Hi baby we don't accept food stamps here
I'll see you later, come by for cookies

I grabbed the milk, put it on the counter,
passed paper shame to the cashier,
squeezed my eyes shut

Coward

Words are harder to dodge
than his left hook would be
Hit me, come on pussy, hit me!
Players at the court's other end
stop dribbling, form a ring
around us   I feel them throb,
hear the hiss of frenzy beg
for blood How easily an elbow
fractures, when you straighten
the arm by the wrist & apply
pressure to leathery flesh
protecting bone   He leans,
shoves me with upturned
palms   I wonder if he knows
eyeballs are softer than eggshells
That a finger jab could make
my face the last image
he'll remember for months
Hit me! What are you a coward? You scared?
I whisper it & almost believe
no one hears but they do
& all go quiet
"Yes, I'm afraid—I'm afraid"
The moment I decide
to suffer or to cause suffering
is quick I turn my head as he
connects, soften the blow
When I see my face in the fear on his
& the weight of my knees push
down on his biceps & I cup his face
with my fingertips like it's some   thing
I've created & the spit is gone
from my mouth, I am afraid

The day a poet I looked-up-to clowned me

He shook my hand so violently
I thought he'd shake me off the map
I just finished saying my last name
when he smiled real big
& nudged me aside
He went to a group of black
students & introduced himself,
I stared at my outstretched hand,
darker than a paper-bag
& lighter than mulch
Oh, you're not Black black?
& I'm cast off
aboard my great-great
grand-pappy's Middle-Passage,
his slaver to the blue-skied,
salt sea air of Caribbean cane-fields
Same all-inclusive package
as our cousins in Virginia
But in this day we are changed,
I am the space left in the wake
of the juke move
he performed to negate me
My blackness & me
shaking hands with the air

Chorus

Mamá Ana:

Ay no, pero

        Isn't poetry about roses are red & violets are blue?

Write about *Quisqueya*, about
our Spanish heritage

No sufrás, hijo.

        James Baldwin: A child cannot afford to be
                 fooled

Casta

Conquistador	Español	Peninsular	Europeo
Colonized	Americano	Indio	Amerindian
Stolen	Slave	Negro	Africano
Español	Colony	Criollo	Colonial
Indio	Español	Mestizo	Rape
Español	Mestizo	Castizo	Pass
Español	Maafa	Colony	Slavery
Africano	Español	Mulato	Rape
Español	Mulato	Morisco	Pass
And	It	Goes	On
Español	Morisco	Chino	
Chino	Indio	Salta Atras	
Salta Atras	Mulato	Lobo	
Lobo	Chino	Gibaro	
Gibaro	Mulato	Albarazado	
Albarazado	Negro	Canbujo	
Canbujo	Indio	Sanbaigo	
Sanbaigo	Lobo	Calpamulato	
Calpamulato	Canbujo	Tente en el aire	
Tente en el aire	Mulato	No te entiendo	
No te entiendo	Indio	Torna atraz	
And	It	Goes	On

Terceron	1/3	Negro	
Quadroon	1/4	Negro	
Quinteroon	1/5	Negro	
Hexadecaroon	1/6	Negro	
Octoroon	1/8	Negro	
Mustee	1/8	Negro	
Mustefino	1/16	Negro	
Griffe	3/4	Negro	
Cafuzo	3/4	Negro	

And   It   Goes   On

Trigueño	Trigueñito	Cimarron
Rojizo	Moreno	Morenito
Quemao	Indiecito	Prieto
Indio	Clarito	Creole
Claro	Oscurito	Blanco
Oscuro	Quemaito	Negro

Fair	Lightskin	High Yellow
Redbone	Olive	Midtone
Brown	Dark Brown	Black

And   It   Goes   On

White (Not Hispanic/Latino)	Black (Not Hispanic Latino)	Native American
White (Hispanic/Latino)	Black (Hispanic/Latino)	Asian (Not Hispanic/Latino)
Asian (Hispanic/Latino)	Two or More Races:	(Not Hispanic Latino)

Chorus

Miguel Piñero:

he said (dips his cigarette)
  he never saw the cause
    but he heard
    the cause

& the Cause was in front of him

      & the Cause was in his skin

          & the Cause was in his speech

             & the Cause was in his blood

seekin' the Cause

while the Cause was dyin' seekin' him   (gestures with cigarette hand,
keeping time with a silent beat)

The Lie

First time we heard the lie I was a little boy   Mrs. Hess, the red-haired landlady, took advantage of any opportunity to ask my grandmother: *Where's the boy's father? & You're his grandmother Where's his grandfather? & Why don't you people ever stay married? & My tax dollars support broken homes like yours with welfare*   Then she'd ask for the rent   My grandmother, tongue unable to lash back, unwilling to do the Tango called English   My grandmother, at a sewing machine eight hours a day, bartending slobs four hours a night, couldn't tell Mrs. Hess where to take herself, my grandmother let Mrs. Hess's tax dollars be praised, she prayed for my dead fathers, poor Mrs. Hess believed the lie & the lie has dogged all my days

Mamá Ana's apartment in Washington Heights

Clang of the police-lock supporting
the door bid us welcome
She'd step just outside it,
the wall behind spared little room
I was stunned
at how leathery & silver she was,
      how compact

We entered the short hallway,
a closet in the middle, door ajar,
too cramped to hang coats
The living room was
the dining room, a film of odorless
      grease cuddled each piece of furniture

Clear plastic over loveseat, sofa,
& arm-chair Oversized sewing machine
by the oversized window
& outside, a fire-escape, where
I drank *café con leche* from a tin cup,
buttered *Yeya* crackers,
      her eyes on me, *come mijo*

We watched movies late night, she talked
through the good parts & nodded off mid-way,
sometimes I'd sneak into her bed,
rats killed time on the kitchen sink,
she'd say, *Lie still & you can stay*
I did & I slept to the echo of her breathing
      bouncing off the close walls

Burn

That winter we learned to play with fire
burning whatever we could find,
our warm breath against cold winds,
coaxing the sparks

Jeffrey, the Frick to my Frack, was afraid,
My daddy told me, we have no business,
as young black men, playing with matches.
Even though you puertirican

The newspaper curled in blue flames,
twisted into white smoke,
I punched him, *I ain't puertirican!*
Besides, it's only paper

We lit whatever we could
We got caught & Mamá Ana told
the neighbors it was a misunderstanding
She beat me with a strap, in the shower, under
a steady stream of hot water

That summer the older boys were burning too
Cursing about cops, *lack of funds,* the power
of the Asiatic black man & how Jesus isn't white
One of them smashed the stain-glass windows
of our church, shouting the same things

Pastor responded with extra collection plates,
Those windows have stood for 60 years!
The congregation gossiped,
All I know is from what little I've seen,
Hagar & Ishmael are black

They were cast out too
Mama Ana whispered in my ear,
They're not in any stain-glass windows either

Bricks *(AKA the Housing Projects)*

Who made these fucking bricks?
Made from despair & fear
Behind these bricks I am hidden

We
are
hidden

Rhonda, she's homeless, she says,
Life is hard on the streets but the streets are free
They can't hide you and they can't hide from you
They have to look at you, even if they ignore you

We
are left
here

Behind these fucking bricks,
only ourselves to meet,

ourselves to beat,

only ourselves
to eat

The dead send dreams

Mamá Ana arrived from the island
a few weeks before her mother would die,
urged by her to leave the deathbed
& come care for us

She died on my birthday
The phone ringing so early
it could only be bad news

I'd been dreaming
I was standing on a crowded sidewalk
with my little cousin Josh
I looked across a six-lane highway
at another crowded sidewalk

We attempted to cross
but Mamá Ana's mother,
screamed from the other side:
No, no cruzes!
& I grabbed Josh's arm

A week or two later
he'd be mauled by a Rottweiler

& survive

Poem for Uncle Jaimé

His big, soft hands had gripped the naked backsides
of the pueblo's many married women
Jaimé Garcia beguiled with blue green eyes—
he was a stone cold fucking machine
& a well mannered mama's boy too
The *viejas* called him gentleman & *bandido*,
he eased up & down the lane, giving kids candy money,
booze to beggars, he even drank Sambuca with the cops
Jaimé crept on your wife as she sat in the shade
drinking *limonáda*, & you, away, working
Pueblo husbands half-suspected the infidelities:
they met & played dominoes to study the facts
It became a club of sorts, each husband pretended:
No, not my wife, passed off fake smiles like hyenas—
the doubt buoyant as a motherfucker
Then *Piel Canela* came to town *Piel Canela*
because she was burnt like sticky cinnamon,
hair & eyes black like shadows in midnight's bedroom
Her teeth flashed wicked   Jaimé passed her gate one day,
saw her bent over, gathering dry palm for a *fogata*—
to keep mosquitoes away   He spoke slick   She finished
his sentences   The fall was quick & the toucans stopped their songs,
the river ceased its dance, & the *viejas* prayed
with *agua florida* soaked rosary beads, & Jaimé barely made it
out of *Piel Canela's* bed before her husband came home
& imagine him, his wife naked in bed, asleep—not yet evening
The feathery hiss of gossip carried him off to the domino club, to rum
Hands smacked domino tables in bitterness: Kill Jaimé Garcia!
Piel Canela's husband said no, that would be too easy,
& pulled a slight hammer from his linen blazer,
a hammer like a child's toy made of wood & metal,
with this, he said, I'll get that bastard   At nights sharp edge
they found Jaimé stumbling drunk along the lane
They beat him, took off his clothes, beat him some more,
& *Piel Canela's* husband came up from behind, held the tiny hammer

69

high up like a testament, & brought it down hard like a judgment
behind Jaimé Garcia's ear   The cry, my God, the cry
After the convalescence, the wives, like roadside flowers, waiting
& Piel Canela, so bold she met him at the gate as nurses walked him in
She searched his eyes for the blue green wildness   Drool
dripped from his lips   He was a boy, a dumb boy

Chorus

Miguel Piñero:

> *and the Cause was dyin' seekin' him*

and the Cause was dyin' seekin' him

> *and the Cause was dyin' seekin' him*
>
> (chuckles, scratches himself)

Mamá Ana speaks on men in power

Será bueno mocharle
los juevos y
darcelas a un perro
con mucha hambre

It would be good to cut
their balls off
and feed them to
a very hungry dog

Elegy Written for the N-word on behalf of the word Nigger by a Nigga
(it's cool man, chill)

1.

Fresh off the boat
Fresh off the plane
Fresh off the islands
& the hurricane rains

just got to the city
& already saying

My neega, my neega
Was good, my neega

Yeah, yeah man,
that's my neega

I be that neega

yeah

Got down with the hustles
Got down with the raps
Got a pair of tims
& a Yankees baseball cap

& you slap neega at the end
of all your sentences
& don't understand
the consequences

2.

X: Wasup my Nigga How you man

Y: Yo man

Z: Oh shit here we go

X: What

Y: Look man Don't call me nigga no more

X: What you talking about man

Z: Told you

Y: I know the truth about it now The hate

X: Nigga how long we known each other What you trying to say

Z: That's what I said B

Y: It's a racist word man Racists use it That cop that slapped me called me a nigger man She wanted to shoot me

Z: I can't be taking responsibility for history Nigga Or for white people

X: Fa real The fuck is wrong with you

Y: I'm woke to it now Can't let it go We gotta do better

X: Ok Malcolm Carlos X I'm gonna say Nigga whenever I want

Z: I'm kinda insulted B   I feel like you calling me a racist and shit

Y: The word is racist man

X: He is calling us racist B

Y: Y'all just don't get it man

X: Oh we get it You the one lost in sauce

Y: Word   How's that

X&Z: Cuz every nigga is a star   every nigga is a star   every nigga is a star

3.

I don't want to be forgotten
I want to be laid to rest

I'm not your intercultural
Metro-card or passport

My name does not prove
your bravery   I am not badge

I do not validate your story,
song, poem or friendships

No, I don't forgive killing
the oppressor   Don't care for *Taking it back*

Never believe no one's listening,
I am not prefix to

bulging crotch, lips, nose, style, ass, hair,
walk, talk, dancing, step or fetch,

I am not a brand or anecdote,
I am not endearment I am hate

I will never be forgotten I
am boogeyman   Who said you can speak for me

Chorus

Mamá Ana:

    (long sigh) *Este mundo*

        se esta

acabando

Irony

for Israeli Minister Eli Yishai
(After the Israeli attacks on illegal African immigrants)

Burning building   Who set the fire   We   Eritrean   Sudanese Darfurians are in it
My wife   Seven months pregnant   Is in it

Who said burn the building   Nazis or Jews / Jews or Janjaweed

Angry mobs   Police mobs   Spit on & beat   We   Eritrean   Sudanese   Darfurians
Women   Children   Bloodied   Condemned

Who urged the beatings   Nazis or Jews / Jews or Janjaweed

Here in the land of Milk & Honey
Here in The Land of Milk & Honey

We are pricked & bleed
We are poisoned & die

> *If we are like you in the rest, we will resemble you in that*

Elegy for Nelson Mandela

For you heaven   will have no walls
will have no doors   no windows or roofs
only parades   people arm in arm

& living   will be an embrace
a reverence   a *How in the world are you?*
a kiss on the lips   intimate & innocent
living breath   & mercy a wild whirlpool

For you heaven,   a nine decade feast
a marquis in gold   *Rolihlahla*- "troublemaker"
a soundtrack: blessed are the stubborn
blessed are they   who have a sense of fairness

of joyful tears   of constant dancing
of humility   of searing passion

For you heaven,   your father's hand
your mother's eyes   a pledge soaked in feather crowns
& you never look down you stopped descending long ago

You won't see   the minstrel show
black face white face happying up oppression
the enemy's death mask they are portraying Mandela

Brother Madibi   you are not Kris Kringle
on a bulging sleigh   bearing gifts for peace
no no no no no   you were militant & ready

You won't see   your long line of enemies
chumps & fools, crying *I loved Mandela! I did!*
Kissing your corpse's ass with one lip
mumbling *Traitor,*   *Communist,* with the other

Art imitating death

Elegy for Israel Hernandez-Llach

1.

Sst. Sst. Sssssssssssssst
Clack clack   Clack
Sssssssssssssst   Sssssssst
Clack   Clack   Clackalackalack

Freeze! Drop the cans &…Hey!!
I said freeze! Go, go! Get the…
Go, go! Radio back up! Go, go!

(pant)

        (pant)

                (pant)

Gotcha! Think it's funny?
To make us chase you?
Hey, no, no, no! Get
back here

(kick)

        (punch)

                (kick)   (punch)

I think this kid needs to relax
I think he needs help relaxing
Get your Taser out

Zzzzzzzap. Zzzzzzzap
Zzzzzzzap. Zzzzzzzap

(high fives) (hooting) (hollering)

Hey   He's not moving

2.

Red left your murdered heart
left the blood of every witness
Red cried *Fuck the flag!*
Red abandoned love
Red hated

Blue fell off veins
fell off police uniforms
Blue cried *Don't call me honor!*
Blue fled courage & crawled
back in the Krylon can you dropped

Yellow could only shine
like gold attracting greed
Yellow cried *Why death, today?*
Yellow stopped the dawn

Green remained green
soaked up every fallen thing
Green cried *Next time, always a next time*
Green changed all colors
Green waited for the rebirth

3.

Important things are invisible
Laws, promises, civil rights,
exist more in the ether
than on paper or in courts,
malleable & based solely
on discretion and hierarchy

What makes an American dream?
How does one become deserving?

Chorus

James Baldwin:

When you're writing

you're trying to find

something which you don't know

The angry Black man

in the room is

invisible—

disarming, disengaging,
        not as dangerous
among the living as in
        the White   of imagination

He be
Sanchez, Johnston, Harjo,
    Patel, & Shabazz,
he tip toe not tap dance,
mumble not mambo,
cry—not rain dance

Let's not simile, or
context the brotha, or—

let's just
piss him, poke him, push him

off
Comportment Cliff,
music his meaning,
        funkify his fight

Knock, knock
Who's there?
Angry Black man
Angry Black man, who?

Me

Chorus

Miguel Piñero:

i dreamt i was this poeta
words glitterin' brite & bold

strikin' a new rush for gold
in las bodegas
where our poets' words & songs

are sung

Mamá Ana:

Write beautiful things, *Mijo*,

only beautiful things

black **Maybe**

The first friend I made in Elizabeth, New Jersey was a white kid named Billy. As a New York transplant my *Dominicano* look wasn't too popular with the Jersey folk. I had an Afro, wore dress pants, a collared shirt, and black leather shoes with little gold buckles. Most of the kids just wanted to know what my thing was. Billy and I couldn't have been more different, but we became close pretty quickly. Despite the fact that Billy's parents wouldn't allow him over my house, my grandmother would allow me over his. She took one look at Billy's blonde hair and blue eyes, and at his mother's middle class American manners, and pronounced their household safe. "Where are you from?" Billy's mother asked, referring to my grandmother's heavy accent. "I thought you were black." On that day I couldn't have imagined how many times I'd have to answer that question. "We're Dominican."

A couple years later, when the neighborhood became predominantly Cuban, African American and Haitian, Billy and his family moved away. My new best friend was black, and his mother wouldn't let him over my house either, on account of us being "Puerto Rican." You can imagine our surprise when I returned with a similar story. My grandmother didn't want me over his house because they were black. We looked each other over. Two skinny round headed, chocolate brown boys wondering what the hell each other's families were talking about. As far as we knew we looked the same. My grandmother was just as black as Tyshaun's mother and I told her as much every time she chided me about playing with him. What was I missing? My aunt took me to black barbershops for shape-ups and number ones. I spent a lot of time at Marvelous Marvin's crying as he picked my tender head before cutting it. Friends called me Del Monte because my head was so peasy. Yet my grandmother believed we were something other than what I was living, what I believed we were: black people who spoke Spanish. I was living a distorted Dominican version of Willie Perdomo's poem "Nigger-Reecan Blues:"

—Hey, Willie. What are you, man? Boricua? Moreno? Que?
 Are you Black? Puerto Rican?
—I am.
—No, silly. You know what I mean: What are you?
—I am you. You are me. We the same. Can't you feel our veins drinking
 the same blood?

—But who said you was a Porta-Reecan?
—Tu no eres Puerto Riqueño, brother.
—Maybe Indian like Gandhi-Indian?
—I thought you was a Black man.
—Is one of your parents white?
—You sure you ain't a mix of something like Cuban and Chinese?
—Looks like an Arab brother to me.
—Naahh, nah, nah. . .You ain't no Porty-Reecan.
—I keep tellin' y'all: That boy is a Black man with an accent.

As I got older I began to recognize the differences between African American culture, Afro-Latino culture, and being black in between. Black being the giant labels America puts on anyone darker than a paper bag. I also knew the word *Negro* well. I'd heard it my whole life in Spanish. What you mean when you say the word *Negro* depends heavily on the modifier because Latinos call each other *Negro* all the time: *Negrito lindo* (black and pretty), *mi Negro* (my black friend/brother), or *maldito Negro* (damned black guy). One thing remained steadfast: my family members never identified themselves as Africa black, and they never spoke about Dominican culture, or Dominican history, as having anything to do with Africa. The phrase *"Tu no eres negro,"* or *"No somos negro,"* was repeated over and over by my grand-uncles, and my grandmother. They'd use slurs like *cocolo*, and *monokiquillo* (basically monkey) when referring to African Americans or other people with strong African features. However, they referred to themselves and to me as *Indio*, a term which means of Indigenous descent. You could say I was more than a little confused growing up, but mostly I was angry. I knew what I saw in the mirror and what I experienced out in the world. Other Latinos repeatedly called me *cocolo*, and white cops called me *darkie* and *nigger*.

I felt like I was living in a perpetual *Twilight Zone* episode. I'm black in a country that by all indications hates black people, and I'm descended from people that are black, but pretend not to be black. Like most teenagers I was too wrapped up in it to see the bigger picture. There was some serious history behind all this un-blackness. And history starts at home.

★

My grandmother, Altagracia Felicia Garcia, was born in Santiago de los Caballeros, Dominican Republic, in 1933. She grew up during the height of Rafael Trujillo's dictatorship. Trujillo ruled the Dominican Republic for thirty years and his mania knew very little boundaries. He was a virulent racist and rapist. Trujillo ordered the deaths of countless Haitians and dark skinned Dominicans in a Hitler-style quest to "whiten" the Dominican Republic. Snitches kept their ears open for three things: anybody disrespecting Trujillo or his regime, young beautiful girls for Trujillo to rape, and confirmation of Haitian blood in the family tree of Dominicans so they could be ripped out by the roots.

Julia Alvarez' novel *In the Time of the Butterflies*, and Junot Diaz' *The Brief Wondrous Life of Oscar Wao* depict snatches of daily life under the regime with particular accuracy. Dominicans living in this atmosphere were paranoid to put it mildly. Some wore makeup to make their complexions appear whiter; families hid their daughters and/or married them off and sent them to the mountains, or out of the country. People were given to spontaneously praising Trujillo in public so others could hear them.

I imagine my grandmother growing up in that country, staring in the mirror everyday, convincing herself she's not black/Haitian, and probably having to convince others. Maybe practicing the word *perejil* (parsley), even though she could roll her *r*'s perfectly, just in case she was put to the test. The French/Creole accent makes rolling the *r* in the Spanish word for parsley, perejil, difficult. The *r* sound comes out like a *th* or more commonly an *l* sound. In 1937, when my grandmother was four years old, Trujillo ordered that all the sugarcane plantation workers along the Dominican/Haitian border be given the parsley test, and those that couldn't pronounce the word were murdered in a massacre that killed thousands of Haitians and dark skinned Dominicans. Edwidge Danticat's novel *The Farming of Bones* is also a powerful and moving dramatization of the massacre, from the perspective of a young Haitian servant girl. Rita Dove also dramatized the Parsley Massacre of 1937 in her poem "Parsley."

> El General has found his word: perejil.
> Who says it, lives. He laughs, teeth shining
> out of the swamp. The cane appears

in our dreams, lashed by wind and streaming.
And we lie down. For every drop of blood
there is a parrot imitating spring.
Out of the swamp the cane appears.

★

Dominican anti-blackness goes back even further than Trujillo's thirty-year reign of terror. During the colonial era, Spaniards set up a naming system called *las castas*, the word *casta* means caste. Under *las castas* Spaniards stood at the top of the social hierarchy, possessing all manner of wealth, power, and influence. As Spaniards copulated with the indigenous and African slave populations (by rape and sometimes, rarely, by marriage) their children were labeled and placed at a certain level within the hierarchy. For example, the child of an African and a Spaniard would be called a *Mulato*. The child of an African and a *Mulato* would be called a *Sambo*. The child of a Spaniard and an Indigenous person was called a *Mestizo*, and on and on. (It is important to note that these are zoological terms applicable to animals.) In order to move up in the social hierarchy everyone needed to be something else. The African or *Negro* wanted to pass as *mulato*, the *mulato* wanted to pass as Spaniard, or *Indio*, and nobody wanted to be *Negro*, black. Under *las castas* Africans were always at the bottom of the pyramid.

Trujillo built his sick twisted rule on top of *casta*. He took the manipulative colonial system of psychological conditioning and self-hate that Dominicans still internalized and magnified it with the power of ten thousand suns. In Trujillo's Dominican Republic denying blackness was life and death. I've heard people who grew up in communist countries tell their horror stories. Secret police picked up them or friends or family members because of an anonymous tip. They were tortured, imprisoned, or killed on the whispered word of some stranger. I think of the generations upon generations of Dominicans living that way, and how the racial/cultural mind fuck Trujillo created has been passed on in the island's DNA. I wonder how much of my grandmother's denial was a self-defense mechanism, how much was self-hate, and how much was just her carrying out what she was taught. After all those years, what did reality have to become.

My grandmother never spoke about her life during the Trujillo era. She owned a *colmado*, or a small grocery store in her village. I know this because when we lived in Harlem she also owned a *colmado* and she would say grocery stores were in her blood. When her Alzheimer's started, little bits of her past would come out unexpectedly, and finally my mother had to tell me the story. My grandmother escaped Dominican Republic after Trujillo was assassinated. Not only was she running from the burning shack, so to speak, she was also fleeing from an abusive husband. He was a tall, blond, honey colored man who owned lots of land, but was quick with his hands. Altagracia was not having that. She hustled her way to New York City carrying at least twenty years of "regime" in her veins, if not more.

★

In 1804 Haiti became the first colony to gain its independence, but independence came at a heavy price. The French repeatedly fought to retake the island, and ultimately forced the Haitian government to agree to a 150-million franc indemnity for the loss of lands and goods. The new Haitian government spread the ideals of freedom from slavery and tyranny. They aided South American revolutionary Simón Bolívar in his efforts to free Colombia and Venezuela from the Spaniards. When the Dominican Republic, then a Spanish colony called Santo Domingo, defeated Spanish colonialists in a revolt in 1821 they sought to unite the island under Haitian rule. For two decades Haiti and the Dominican Republic were one country, Spanish Haiti, but the economic yoke around Haiti's neck made sustained unification impossible. In 1844, in response to extreme taxation, Dominicans rebelled against the Haitians and established the Dominican Republic. You know the old saying; no good deed goes unpunished.

Since that time Haiti has struggled through some form or another of crushing international debt, economic stagnation, or government corruption. During Trujillo's rule all these different layers of history, colonialism, racism, massacres, corruption, and Haiti's perpetual economic hardships cemented a hate/hate relationship between the two countries.

★

As a child of Dominican immigrants I can say that my grandmother's people are suffering from serious ignorance. A kind of Stockholm syndrome, when a victim captured, abused, traumatized or beaten by a captor, begins to sympathize and empathize with that captor, exists within the Dominican Republic. They empathize; sympathize even, with *casta*, and the legacy of black hatred Trujillo left for them. Recently, the Dominican Republic's constitutional court passed a law stripping citizenship from thousands of Dominicans born of one or more Haitian parents. The spirit of the law seems to be geared towards deporting illegal Haitian immigrants, however, the fact is that for many born in poor rural and urban areas, documentation of births, deaths and when and where their ancestors entered the country is shaky at best.

Poverty and fear of deportation makes it difficult for Dominico-Haitians to prove their status. The situation is exacerbated by mob violence. Dominicans are roaming villages and cities, grabbing Haitians and dark-skinned Dominicans and brutalizing them. There has been at least one confirmed lynching. Bill Fletcher Jr. recently discussed this issue on his YouTube program The Global African. He noted that advocates of Dominico-Haitians are concerned because "it appears that the mechanism to identify possible deportees will be based off physical appearance. Specifically, dark skinned individuals."

I've read articles expressing outrage over what has been dubbed *La Sentencia*. Social media is buzzing with links, videos, and heated conversations. I also know that the United States has been conducting similar deportations. In fact, I'd be willing to wager that the Dominican constitutional court took their cue from us. Illegal immigrants and their children, children born and raised in America, have been deported back to their parents' country of origin. Some of these children don't even speak the language, usually Spanish. However, the US government has sent them packing, no questions asked, United States citizens. The Huffington Post reports that, "When a parent is deported, their U.S.-born children sometimes leave with them. But some stay in the U.S. with another parent or family member. Some children end up in U.S. foster care." In 2013, more than 72,000 illegal immigrants with American-born children were deported.

It used to be that if you were an illegal immigrant and your child was born in this country, you were given legal residency, and you were given a green card. That doesn't appear to be the case any longer.

★

Here's some hard shit for people to deal with, especially Latinos. I love *bachata, salsa, merengue*, rice and beans. I grew up watching annual reruns of *Roots*, every episode of *Diff'rent Strokes*, dancing along with Michael Jackson, rapping Public Enemy's lyrics, and I rocked a Gumby and a high top fade when that was the style. None of these loves was or is mutually exclusive of the others. Growing up I identified (and still do) with black culture, arts, music, fashion, everything, because that's what we looked like, what we are, not African American, but black.

This is not to say that there's some formulaic definition of blackness, or what Amiri Baraka called "a static cultural essence to blacks." There is not. Neither is blackness that marketable, sellable product or anger Claudia Rankine criticizes Hennessy Youngman for pushing, in chapter two of *Citizen: An American Lyric*:

> On the bridge between this sellable anger and "the artist"
> resides, at times, an actual anger. Youngman in his video
> doesn't address this type of anger: the anger built up
> through experience and the quotidian struggles against
> dehumanization every brown or black person lives simply
> because of skin color.

God forbid blackness should ever be described as Rachel Dolezal. Instead, I think of Aimé Césaire's *Negritude* "...the awareness of being black, the simple acknowledgment of a fact which implies the acceptance of it, a taking charge of one's destiny as a black man [person], of one's history and culture." We must take Negritude beyond the borders of literary movements and make "taking charge" part of our very fabric.

In high school I rarely got along with the Dominicans that had just arrived to America. They watched me suspiciously, my slang, my easygoing nature with black, white, gay, and straight. The fact that my best friend was black, and that the rest of my crew consisted of Cuban, Colombian, Puerto Rican, Filipino, and Ecuadorian, was a big bone of contention for the new arrivals. Something about the way I carried myself troubled my *paisanos* and there was no going back. I was called a fake Dominican on several occasions, and I relished the role of outcast. My motto was "fuck your racist bullshit. You don't even know your history."

Perhaps they didn't yet understand that America thrusts black or white upon you quickly, you have to decide, you have to know who and what you are. Life in Dominican Republic had been too culturally ignorant and insular. Meanwhile in America, some euro-centric or Castilian Latinos are passing for white, but Afro-Latinos are either self-hating or catching hell or both, or just plain confused about who the hell they are. Most of the Dominicans I know have a discernable African lineage, but too many are quick to claim Latin American status as opposed to Afro-Caribbean identity. Let's be honest, Cuba, Puerto Rico, Dominican Republic, and Haiti aren't in South or Central America, they're in the Caribbean. We need to re-examine our historical cultural selves. I completely agree that race is a construct, but identity is a necessity.

I've met a lot of European immigrants in America, both first and second generation. They come to America and assimilate quickly into white culture. The children of African diaspora, for complex reasons, have some difficulty owning our blackness. Yes, history has a lot to do with it; what our families teach us also has a lot to do with it. We must overcome these factors, educate ourselves, and become a part of the larger conversation, the critical one about how much Black Lives Matter. They're killing us out here, and in places like the Dominican Republic, we're killing each other.

★

In his essay "Encounter on the Seine: Black Meets Brown," James Baldwin explores differences between the American children of African diaspora and their colonial cousins; Antiguans, Martiniquais, and St. Lucians, just to name a few. Perhaps the most critical peculiarity Baldwin observes is the African American disconnect from a black nation, the loss of black hegemony, and the resulting psychological trauma.

> The African before him has endured privation, injustice, medieval cruelty; but the African has not yet endured the utter alienation of himself from his people and his past…and he has not, all his life long, ached for acceptance in a culture which pronounced straight hair and white skin the only acceptable beauty (38).

Isn't this a derivative of the Haitian/Dominican struggle? Haiti is strongly tethered to its past, to its identity as a nation comprised of children from Africa, while the Dominican Republic is trying to be anything but. The Dominican idea of identity and beauty and acceptance is rooted in euro-centric ideas of beauty.

My grandmother, our extended family, and Dominicans I know have taught me that changing hearts and minds is difficult work. It takes time, but it also requires revelatory experiences, and forging new memories that can smooth the scar tissue of old traumas. Unfortunately, Haitians and their Dominican-born children don't have that kind of time. My individual effort at accepting my blackness, my history, and my attempt to build a way forward isn't helping them.

But America and the Civil Rights movement have taught me that I have options. I can exercise my political power by writing a petition asking the President of the United States to pressure the Dominican government to ensure that the rights of Dominicans born of Haitian descent are protected. And that Haitians facing legal deportation are not butchered or beaten in the streets. This petition should demand that our President threaten to cut off aid and issue sanctions if the Dominican Republic does not comply. I can reach out to my local and state representatives and ask them to support the petition. I can use my social media presence and challenge friends, family, and celebrities to put their names behind it.

Just as importantly, I can tell my story, the truths I've pieced together from history's lies. If you're white, take what you've learned from this essay and put your privilege to work. I don't mean that disrespectfully, honestly. If you're like me, black, Dominican, American, and you love your Dominican grandmother or mother, even though they talk that shit you can't wrap your head around, seek the knowledge and then educate them, whether they like it or not. Start the process of figuring out how the Dominican American experience can help island Dominicans get their lives together. Start the conversations that can actively inform the Afro-Latino experience and the Afro-Caribbean identity. How does the Afro-Latino/Caribbean experience in America mirror the African American experience for you? We need to talk about this. In time, these conversations can help all Dominicans to be more like our Haitian brothers and sisters, proud to walk black and beautiful in the sun.

[Elegies]

Mixtape for City Kids from Dysfunctional but Happy Families, Kids Like Me *(a new form)*

When the light from that moon spilled
out of your mother's belly, I tell you,
you were smiling then. We need a name:
but we can't call this *Menace to the Hood*
or *Boys in Society* or no shit like that. You
have been born into a world. Look around.
See that black boy over there running scared,
his old man got a problem & it's a bad one. Mami?
Even though she don't have a job, Mami still
works hard. The last 23 years of her life have been
spent teaching a poet & killing generations
of cockroaches with sky-blue plastic slippers.
These are the people who will love you
with the same love they received, or hopefully
better. You will have enemies too. My enemies
ride jets to parties. They use words like casualties
to speak of murder. Yes, you'll survive. Look at me.
I'm shocked too, I'm supposed to be locked up too,
you escape what I escaped you'd be in Paris
getting fucked up too. My father said…surviving
one thing means another comes & kills you.
He's dead, & so, I trust him. I know this isn't much.
But I wanted to explain this life to you, even if
I had to become, over the years, someone else to do it.
The miracle of Jesus is himself, not what he said or did
about the future. Forget the future. I'd worship someone
who could do that. Then, slowly, Lo is fo e ri bari
Lo is fo e ri bari love is for everybody Love is for
every every body love love love everybody love.

This moment / Right now
—*for Monica Hand*

there's a whispered prayer blowing
the crumbs of a season's harvest
off a girl's plate

& a roar breaks from her insides,
the roar a lioness
a beast that knows

& a man kneels somewhere
cupping his tears
      for the loneliness he feels

though he's surrounded by the world,
& a finch in a tree singing
for a lover as the buds on its branch

pop into leaves that will flourish
& welcome the green grasses.
Right now, a boy is wondering

if people can really dodge bullets
& is he one of them & somewhere nobody bothers
to ask, they simply wait.

Wind spins across the landscape
they say God is twirling his fingers—

The heartbroken hook new bodies,
night after night, drink after drink

& I dance—my feet mashing grapes
for wine & I sing mockingly—
      what is life / what is life?

A Love Poem Post Love

I don't want to be afraid to love
I want to know where to love from.

The heart, everyone says—please,
the heart is made of sand, crafted
by children pretending on a beach,
today buried in it tomorrow small hands
& starfish stencils erased by the sea.
& on it goes, forever changing. I'm
going to love from the soles of my feet
from every place I've ever been,
the supermarket parking lot, prison,
the dance floor, my vegetable garden,
all the kitchens, the beds & dream veils,
so that when I enter my beloved all that I am
enters with me & all my beloved is
enters me—this is how I want to know
love—through the gentle pain of experience,
because birds never ask *is this song* rivers
never ask *is the ocean this way*.

Cento for a Mood

This is the way to achieve immensity. My voice
is in the woods; my hands are in the water. To crawl
deep into memory, to step into the cellar & wipe
with one's sleeve what must fight off reclamation.
Such stupid beauty, beauty you can stick a manicured
finger into & through, beauty that doesn't rely
on any sentence the sun chants. Our world survives
on two things: first the poet & second the poet. & if sun
comes How shall we greet him? Exhaust the little moment.
Sadder than water & sand & palms. From water comes
the anguish of clouds. If you can't be free, be a mystery.

Elegy for Bill Withers

After the breakup—
me & my daughter's mother burned as acid burns.

The pickup for weekend visitation—combustible.

Our tensions weren't the worst thing—how it weighed
on our daughter—dragged her joy down
to the soles of her Kimpossible sneakers.

The handoff [court language] a kerosene dream,
slick shit falling from her Mama's mouth.
I wouldn't spark it—not this joker, not most days.

Me & my baby girl—we out—just the two of us making
small-talk in the elevator, then out through the building's doors
& in the car—buckled in—on the radio:

Just one look at you / & the world's alright with me
Just one look at you / & I know it's gonna be
A lovely dayyyyyyyyyyyy

& just like that we're singing & laughing
& there's no impossible days & joy rises
from the soles of her Kimpossible sneakers
& escapes as the truest voice I've ever heard
& we are sky & free, we are love.

To A Young Man on His First Period

The way my matriarchs sat at the table
that morning is a panorama in my mind.

Tía Nereida sitting cross-legged, pushing
back the hair from her forehead
& holding the cup in meditation.

Mami cradling *un cafécito* with one hand,
her other arm across her chest—hand resting
on her arthritic shoulder & my big sister

Judy—for whom not enough *platano maduros*
existed in the world on that morning,
& I was welcomed as a hero when I sat

down to eat my Frosted Flakes.
Apurate papi, pa que vayas a la bodega,
a five-dollar bill pushed at me.

Acuerdate, Kotex, ok, Kotex, *no tenga pena.*
At the *bodega*—I passed the purplish-blue package.
El bodegero looked at me long & hard.

Wasup macho-man? You good *hombre*?
& older boys walked in & saw & hungered:
I know what that is—open it—gimme one!

& there was no way—so a fat bloody lip,
two scraped knees & a headknot later
I made it home—the package unopened.

Judy pinched my chin up to see my lip.
Did you get yours in too, did you fight back?
She ran warm water over my lip, & I nodded yes.

Bueno, she replied, *in this life
we all got to bleed sometime.*

Elegy for my Pop

In the dream he gasped for breath.
I sat bedside & he reached for my hand.
We accepted the dream's tenderness.
In the real world we don't know each other,
& he says as much.

This dream—I'm an unknown man gifting
forgiveness to an unknown man.

Pop, what can you do? Life is like that
sometimes, rest easy, I say—*rest.*

He died like the sun breaking clouds
over 161st St & Broadway.

Charge that to the Game

I wonder what happened to the baby.
I mean, after the mom slipped her crack
vials into the baby's diaper—I never went back.

I copped a dime bag & ran to School 3,
looked for my crew, the night ugly, I sat
on bleachers under a streetlight.

No one around, rain cut silence, soaked
my Philly, I couldn't roll the blunt, damn.
Scoped 5-0 circling the park—I ate the weed

& walked home—by the end
I was floating, tried sneaking in but
my sister Kyana posted at the kitchen table.

Eating a dime bag of weed hits different.
Kyana eyeballed me—I played it cool,
served my rice, black beans & steak & sat

down to eat in the smoothest move since
silk came on the scene. *So wassup?* she asked.
Chillin, I replied—& shoved a forkful

into my mouth, a short trip, since my chin
dipped in the plate & by the time I realized
Kyana laughed so hard she had tears in her eyes. I kept

going with it—she laughed like a baby when
a parent acts funny, so I did it again,
my face in the plate as I pushed food into my mouth.

She laughed like a baby—I was high as a kite
& she laughed & laughed like a baby—a baby.

A Tempest

1

My father decided I would be born at sea
thirsty & surrounded by the risk of drowning.

My father was a great sailor, a seaman, navigated
only the darkest waters—the sweetest squalls

which is to say he was a drinker, like his father
before him, & now I had to learn the rhythm of the waves,

how a full moon makes water bulge, makes high & low tide.
I had to learn to follow stars home to strange ports.

My father decided I would be born at sea,
so he left me in a dugout—the shoreline nowhere in sight.

Thank god for the saints—those monoliths on land
light towers on the sea & eagles in the sky

which is to say thank god for mamás, tías & abuelas,
where would the wandering sailor babies float to without them.

Blessèd be these lights who did their own time on the sea
who enjoyed a storm or two before the warm hearth of a slick boatsman

who pay their penance as watchers of the sailor's bastards
who drink tears & listen to boleros on Friday & Saturday nights

& yell & scream at us as if we were those lost sailors
& love & protect us as if we were those lost sailors.

2

My mother prayed I would be born on earth
muddy in a soil I could mold into stones & mountains.

My mother was born in sky & reigned over earth & sea,
but alone & above it all her power—all about her.

She bird's eye view, she omniscient narrator,
she howled winds laying waste to all in her wake.

Kindling love anger tenderness & home into fire
then blowing ash up & darkening the sky

which is to say she felt powerless in all her power
which is to say I was a babe in the eye of the storm.

The sea gives of itself to the sky & waits for rhapsody
blue when passive & gray when roiling & vexed.

My mother wore a dress made of hurricanes
& my father sang a tidal wave of boleros.

Dear mother & father what have you made what exactly
was the plan when you collided across nature?

3

When the sailor's song charms all the sirens
red wine seas taste so wrong & so good.

When rum rivers run brown like cane sugar
when deep oceans burn splashed foams of vodka

the sailor believes he's solved a riddle,
he swims carelessly & loses sight of the boat

which is to say that my father found refuge in bottles
the green ones—ancient messages—were his favorite.

Whatever waters he entered he'd swim in
until his heart was heavy as a whale & leaking.

All of this happened under the sky.
The bottle's patina could not hide the handsome sailor,

its curves echoed his charming song on the spray
& on the wind & way up to the sky went his song.

When have the sirens threatened to drown themselves?
On that day, after the sailor spurned them & longed for sky.

4

In human form they made love on the dance floor.
Dressed in white linen & hats like pampas leaves.

There is a feeling beyond jealousy beyond envy
amidst the tenements the avenues & the night clubs.

They were no longer sailor & sky they dripped
swagger & love & joy & swaying hips & tongues.

All wanted to stand & dance in their light.
They are here   people cried   *They are here.*

The sailor & the sky owned the city & all in it,
owned each other. To own a thing tests your love of a thing

which is to say that for my father & mother
it would never be enough. They needed ruin.

5

There is a feeling beyond jealousy beyond envy.
I'll repeat this. It is true. Always present & close.

The sun watched my mother & father during the day.
The moon watched my mother & father during the night.

Arrogant sailor thought the sun. *I burn next to her daily.*
If she wills a breeze over the trees, I warm it.

I shine upon the waters.   I illuminate.
The sky is mine. She is mine. She is mine.

Arrogant sailor thought the moon.   *I sit near her nightly.*
If she wills a wave on the waters, I make it sparkle.

I shine upon the waters.   I illuminate.
The sky is mine. She is mine. She is mine.

Which is to say that my mother had her pick, day
& night the sailor's treasured sky was longed for & desired.

She loved the smell of spirits & salt on his breath
the cool heat of his skin like swimming under the sun all day

which is to say my mother loved my father like no other,
but there is a feeling beyond jealousy beyond envy.

Who lied first the sun the moon? No one remembers.
The sea washed away the hangers on the *farandula.*

In the aftermath the sun did not rise for days so it could not set.
The moon lost all memory & was ragged & stoic ever after

which is to say my mother & father accused each other of infidelity.
A force of nature annihilates the landscape. What could two of them do?

6

The moon was a slim pretty boy named *Pablito*.
He moved like silk in the wind. Smelled like burning incense.

He was lusted after almost as much as my father. Almost.
When the Moon looks down at its silver glow

kissing everything it doesn't want to come in second.
He shined his brightest shine & stepped to the sky.

He was milky he was glaze & poured butter for many nights.
Who lied first? No one remembers. The way I heard it

the sky wasn't interested. She turned this way & that way
which is to say my mother turned him down quicker than quick

but a lie doesn't need good soil good light or fresh water.
A lie only needs someone to believe it & the sailor believed.

When has the sea pulled down the moon & beat it
pounded it in the waves & drowned it free of its memory?

It was on that night. Lie or no lie the moon had it coming.
The sailor drifted under a darkened sky for many nights.

7

The sun was a mean son of a bitch.
There's no other way to say it.

He will not be named here. He happened.
His role will be told. That's all the history he gets.

History believes people worshipped the sun.
In truth they feared it. Good sun brings crops.

Good Sun brings golden skin. Too much sun
scorches earth dries rivers & seas & brings drought.

The sun chased the sky with a fury that made everybody suffer.
His lust a wilting razing thing, but his lust had limits.

The sun only gets a set number of hours a day.
He rises & does his thing, but he must set,

which is to say that this man worked quick & hard,
which is to say he had an in. He knew my father.

The sky wasn't interested she turned him that way & this way
which is to say my mother turned him down quicker than quick.

But sun left a wound. A hate. The sailor floated on the sea
in the heat of the sun & this was a betrayal, it burned.

The sea cannot grab the sun alone. It needs help.
How the sailor used eclipse & damped sun's power nobody knows.

Which is to say my father set him up,
which is to say my father shot that man & almost killed him.

When does the sun miss work?
When does the sun not shine in the sky?

When love is not enough.
When what you need is ruin.

8

What does a pregnant sky look like
after the wrath after the terrible loving?

How does she carry, who rubs her swollen feet,
how does sky hold water & child & kicks?

She pours oceans onto earth. She purges
all the waters ever gave her all the sailor ever gave

which is to say my mother could keep no food down,
which is to say the sailor watched it all from a boat.

He never returned to the sidewalks, the tenements.
His ruin was forever. He left his boat adrift & swam away.

O the storm raged & rightly so. What now?
What to do with this child & the flooded landscape?

Let it rain sky wept. Let it rain forever if it must.
Let the tides rise & rise & my sailor, be gone.

Elegy in the Key of Life
—a bop for e.l.

Beloved, your absence—bouquet of loss.
Chrysanthemum & lily flower salver—my grief
a beast center stage—you are dead.
Beloved, I meant to call, to visit, that's my excuse.
I'm spinning a little life, the one you tired of—opted out of
on your own terms— I believe I would have changed your mind.

Love's in need of love today / Don't delay / Send yours in right away

Grief jumps at me—shadow in the ruins of your last words:
Just pray for me—you are always a sweetheart to me!
I have kneaded & knuckled your words for days.
Beloved, I'm stuck in the creases.
Night bends & arcs in a world without you.
Light yearns to ripple in the form of memory.
I am soaked in disbelief—overrun in tears—a fake stoic.

Just pray for me—you are always a sweetheart to me!

Love's in need of love today / Don't delay / Send yours in right away

Beloved, death has a way of hoarding the grief-stricken sigh
& I used to believe I knew what you might have wanted.
I flip through conversations, texts, emails & voicemails
& I hear it over & over again—peculiar goodbye so different
from the spelling of your name—from your lowercase preference.
Be Happy, you would say—*Be Happy*, with an exclamation mark.

Love's in need of love today / Don't delay / Send yours in right away

"The ocean pours through a jar...it swims inside the fish"
—Rumi

...maybe then I can walk down to the port
jump in the Atlantic, sink to the bottom
& walk underwater all the way to the Caribbean,

the sea telling its stories as I cross over
into the land of the dead, no need to dream,
water is the doorway between worlds.

...maybe then a stairwell opens in the wet
earth & as I descend, I become dirt & me
& my ancestors have a séance in the soil

& like a geyser, ancestors lift me high
into the sky dressed in bone white pants,
shirtless & barefoot shouting birdsong.

...maybe it's too soon for this kind of talk,
plenty of sun, sea, & grass right in front of me
plenty of the living & dead right in front of me.

Mixtape for City Kids from Dysfunctional but Happy Families, Kids Like Me *(B-side)*

But it's hard isn't it? Not to perform what they say
about our sadness, when we are always so sad.
When are we not grieving? Not to be all suffering
& pain define me, but a man sings by opening his mouth
a man sings by opening his lungs by turning himself into air.
When a girl pronounces her own name there is glory when
a woman tells her own story she lives forever.
Jesus the air is so thick & I'm drowning in my own sight
in the bright black streets in the dawn breaking
like riptides. I have no desire to make you "tough" or "street,"
perhaps because any "toughness" I garnered came reluctantly.
Dread stalks our streets & our faces. Time is not money. Time is time.

There is a House

There is a house
with all the rooms filled with Momma
but there is a river
that separates me from this house
it is a wide river
a river so wide that
it must be called a sea
yes, a sea
a sea so wide
that it must be called time
yes, time
a time so wide
that it must be called death
yes, death

—Lamont B. Steptoe

Elegy in which grief sends me

in search of dream in search of amber
& pounding a sandalwood tambourine
to soothe fellow travelers in the dark.
Mami, when I journey backward I leave
the lamp—so much of life is seeing,
& memory— that blind knife thrower—
demands faith, nakedness, open hands held
softly against the heart—I'm searching
for wonder, & *from*, for womb, & *from*
for the melting candlewax of mothersong.
I mimic the song as best I can hoping
to hear a chime echo back in the dark
but even the sweet runnel of darkness is tiring.
Mami, I look at what I'm running from,
the palatial estate burning inside me
the world wants me to ignore it.
I realize that to remember is to grieve
so I wiggle the tambourine,
I am my own parade steadily advancing
chanting—tambourine slapping my thigh.
The grief, so terribly long—remembers
the greed, so terribly long—remembers
& the *chint chint* of my tambourine breaks.

Elegy in which you & the wind whisper to me

Gather up my ashes you say—in the dying howl's echo
wind brings your voice & snatches your body away.
This long night—pissed off guitar & bourbon—neat—long,
mourning in darkness on a sofa while the house settles long.
Mami—we can't keep having these conversations.
Gather up my ashes you say—dust tickles my nose
the wind brings your voice & muffles my prayers,
tears & spit cull in my palms—slide down my wrists.
Mami—what you will think of me, I can't listen.
I bend like a tree limb as wind pushes your whispers
into my ears on my knees silent & whimpering like a madman.
Gather up my ashes you say—*in a whoosh I'll be gone.*
In a whir I hear over & over again. In a whoosh. In a torment.

Elegy in which we are quantum theory

Mami, you are an object in space pulling me,
I must finish out this life—Mami, life is a field
of magnetic & electric waves propelling us all.
Mami, I am a marmalade of particles you called
Negrito lindo—& in a quantum blink
the particles you've become & my yet to be particles
will float along on waves of gravity & then, Mami
we'll drink *café con leche* with *cassava*
& all the while—the universe crackling—
like an old radio playing *boleros*.

Elegy in which math proves the dead are better off without us

Reality is a network of granular events.
Space, time, matter, & energy all melt into probability.

Mami, observe this equation:
love + comfort = familiarity ÷ neglect = mistakes
Or this one: loss x regret x grief = suffering

It is highly probable I fucked up towards the end
which is to say I believe you know this but

      Y   o

              u

       A   r   e

S   t   a   r

     D   u   s   t

   N   o   w

You singing & dancing in subatomic chaos.
You better for leaving us.
You particles in perpetual motion.
I inert in melancholy math & elegiac equations:

death x (p) ÷ elegies = loss ∞

Elegy in which is hidden an ode to your beehive updo

What does a Caribbean woman free from the shackles
of Trujillo & machismo dream upon stepping
foot in New York City? In the photo you are kneeling,
one arm across your thigh & the other holding your purse,
staring past the cameraman into a future you couldn't possibly
know would include me, your oldest daughter's son—stuck
on you & I don't know the appeal of a beehive updo
except that you look so beautiful, so confident, so like me when
I'm wearing new sneakers & starting out in the evening.
Mami, if you only knew there's a pants suit revolution happening
now but you were rocking pants suits in the 60's with beehive updos
& platform shoes & as I burn a hole in this crinkly sepia photo, seeking
details within details I wish I could just pick up a phone & ask
you to head over to Wal-mart with me & we could laugh at the fake updos
on sale & I'd take advantage of the moment to say no one rocked it like you.
A different kind of crown for a new freedom—for a new queen.

Elegy in which I wrestle the 800lb gorilla

Air escapes my lungs in a long high-pitched wheeze.
I am losing badly & perhaps even giving in.
There is a state I'm trying to reach where in between
consciousness & unconsciousness you move
into the afterlife—& then back again. I go limp,
let the gorilla put me in a colossal clutch,
it is sweet oblivion & I see you there nodding no.
Mami, I've stolen a word & it's brought me closer
to you—& Mami, you won't believe the irony.
The word is *goya*—please laugh, we used Goya products
all the time, *goya*, it is Urdu for a fantasy so realistic
one suspends belief in reality—Mami,
I will fight this silverback the rest of my life
suspended in his bristly arms—between life & death
& watching your face nodding no, no.

Elegy in which I rename a city for you

because the bric a brac & cracked curbs,
because the buildings & stoops,
because your freckled cheeks & tough smile.
All of New York must say your name & know it is home:
La Isla de La Altagracia.

All of New York must wrestle the letters in your sweet name,
feel the cottonmouth, New York will sing the song of my grief
La Isla de la Altagracia,

& New York I rename *La Isla de La Altagracia*
& Brooklyn I rename *La Isla de La Altagracia*
& Queens I rename *La Isla de La Altagracia*
& the Bronx I rename *La Isla de La Altagracia*
& Staten Island I rename *La Isla de La Altagracia*
& Long Island I rename *La Isla de La Altagracia*
& London becomes—*La Isla de La Altagracia*
because you loved to watch Benny Hill
& you loved James Bond & Mami—the little blue dot in space
I rename *La Isla de La Altagracia.*

Now, come back Mami—I have repeated your name
enough times to conjure you.

Elegy in which I recall being told you were dying

I was on the terrace, wrestling with the moon
or dropping my daughter off at kindergarten.
My aunt's panicked voice a fat heart stuck in her throat
& I carried the moon on my back to the hospital.

I was on the terrace, wrestling with the moon
or stuck in a nightmare—the closer I moved
to the hospital door, the further away it ran.
I crashed sidewalk window & wall, moon on my back.

I was on the terrace, wrestling with the moon
or calcified when my aunt cried, *She died—she died.*
Mami, your skin was cold & still soft
& your freckles like the shadows on the moon.

I was on the terrace, wrestling with the moon
or staring like a fool into the blue silk of night's skirt
while the loom making life's fine muslin broke
& the moon offered only the cold silver of struggle.

Elegy in which I hide an elegy in a ghazal for Syria

It is true—I've thought only of your death,
& then the *Daily News* cover featured a young boy's death.

Alzheimer's didn't kill him—that slow chewing Boa constrictor.
There is a tyrant named Assad in Syria & he gassed the boy to death.

On pages 4 & 5 countless children were arrayed like meat at market
& strangely, selfishly even Mami—I thought only of your death,

of you in that coffin & your jaw askew same as the children in the paper.
You are not those children—I am not that far gone amidst death

& yet I wail, their parents wail, Allah! We cry, Allah! In my grief
I wake up I go to work I drink my coffee I sleepwalk in death.

Mami—I cried for those children—I cry for you—I am an ocean.
Dirt makes me sick ash makes me sick ashes to ashes dirt to death.

Everyone is dying—the *Daily News* called 2016 the Grim Reaper.
The whole world is grieving & I think only of your death.

Elegy in which I explain the end of the world to a ghost

Mami, today they killed people with the mother of all bombs.
A Facebook post cried that they've conflated birth with death.
All I know is that there are countless mourners like me in Afghanistan.
Mami, remember my 2nd grade school picture? My buckteeth
out of control, my pale blue button up shirt, the kind I still own
I used to say I want to be Cobra Commander, to rule the world
& you never asked why. Every day I watch us spiral to apocalypse.
Mami, in some hidden room in some hidden mansion the end
has been decided, there's a plan we know nothing about.
When I earned my HS diploma there was a shadow over everything.
The fork in the road was all you thought about while I wanted control
& decades later, on what was maybe my proudest day, your daughter,
my mother stared up into my face, surprised & proud at my success.
Mami, perhaps 20 years from now I'll rule this failing world.
I'll bring it back from the brink like a despot whose sins are washed
away because he survived & rewrote history, or I'll pass
in the slaughter & we'll have this conversation face to face,
imagine what that photograph will look like.

Elegy in which I dream of us under fruit trees

I was writing at an old splintered table under an apple tree.
Apples kept falling all over & there were other trees:
orange trees, pear trees, avocados, & fruits kept falling.
Mami, you entered through a door I hadn't seen before.
Look at all this fruit I said, *look Mami, here try some.*
You ate from my hand & we laughed but I was anxious,
I had to get back to my writing—the page iridescent.
You cupped my face & said *Escribe mijo, vete,* & folded
your skirt & filled it with fruit & I watched you walk
out the door as I wrote & wrote & wrote myself awake.

Elegy in which I consider the resurrection

Scholars say the bible is written in parables,
that it uses symbolic language to explain life,
choices measured against infinity—clouds of dust
struggling up the mountain—three days to return
to leave again in a blink, time enough
to inspire the faithful, to spread the gospel, give hope.
Mami, you died over a month ago so I'm calculating
we all are—three days, years, decades or cycles of the moon
or as the crow flies, the horse rides, the wind affects the tides.
Our grief is a house of mirrors—what would you say
if you rose pristine from the ashes & saw us in our silos
each one believing their grief to be the alpha & omega.
Mami, I think I understand why resurrection is brief—
no need to stick around & see the same stuff again.

Elegy in which I buy my Uber driver a pint of gin

Mami, only because you'd say to me,
in your deepest Celia Cruz gravel,
You must live like a man. A man! did I realize
the driver was asking me what was wrong.
I sighed, he asked, *Long night?*
I said *Yeah man & the bourbon here is twice
as much as three drinks at my hotel.*
Shit, he replied, *we can stop at the sto'
it's on the way.   Fa real?* I asked.
Look man, he said, *I'm here to help.*
Mami, this was man to man.
Before I got out I asked, *You need something?*
& he hesitated. *I got you* I said. *Well,* he replied,
a pint of New Amsterdam gin would be alright.
New what? I asked. *I'll come with you,* he said.
On the way back I held on to both bottles.
We pulled up & I gave him the gin—he nodded.
You'll work that out, he said without saying.

Elegy in which "Happy" by Pharrell sends me spiraling

Mami, I'm doing Couch to 10K because I've let myself go
& it is best to get back into these things slow & because
I'm seeking the untainted joy of sweat & endorphins
& the song changes & I'm asked to clap along if I feel—
& I do. I see us dancing in the kitchen—even Alzheimer's
couldn't steal the words to your favorite *bachatas*
or steal the muscle memory of your easy two step,
& was I happy because I remember us dancing,
was I happy because you never forgot how to dance
was I happy because you never forgot how to sing
or was I happy because in those ten fog filled years
you were happy all the time & unaware of how we clapped
along to any glimpse of the old you.

Elegy hidden inside an ode to beauty

The minute we are born death starts ticking
& for the longest time we can't see it.
Mami, it's the sheen—it fools us all.
I ran my hands through the grass & weeds today
& told my landscaper to make it beautiful
or to kill the weeds—he told me his brother
is in jail for six months, *At least it's not years*
I said. Mami—he'll miss the summer & face
two winters back to back with no respite.
There are buds on my grapevines—so soon.
The citrus tree did not recover & chickweed
have taken over the yard & I'm staring at one spot
under the beech tree, where I'd put out a chair for you
half in the shade & half in the sun, you will not see it again.
Today after ordering the weeds killed I sat at my desk
my youngest daughter walked the dog with my mother in law.
Mami, you do not know her, but after, she rumbled into the room
& smiled—*I have a surprise for you Papi*—& gave me a dandelion.

Note to AB (A Boogeyman)
—for Amiri Baraka

Everybody digs a Boogeyman, baby.
The people need a monster to fear
to pull the blanket over their eyes & hide
from—Boogeyman hand poking out
from dark neo-liberal closets.

Everybody digs a Boogeyman, baby.
Who they want to hate you.
Why they want you hated.
How they want you hated.
What you do to be hated.

Get down boogie oogie oogie—

Hide truth & a couple buildings collapse
Government will say Boogeyman did that.
Tell truth in a poem when a couple buildings collapse
Governor will call you a Boogeyman for that.
Everybody digs a Boogeyman, baby.

I am I am the most beautiful Boogeyman—

Variation on Lines of Dialogue from Bill Murray's Groundhog Day

Well, what if there is no tomorrow? There wasn't one today.
—Phil Connors, Groundhog Day

I used to ride on the back of Miguelito's bike, not pulling
on his shoulders as he pedaled. Back then, even the burning skulls

of dead apartment buildings seemed beautiful—we never said,
thought, or dreamed tomorrow—today replayed every day.

★

No matter how often I opened & closed the fridge:1 ketchup packet,
1 egg, 1 carton of OJ 3 days expired—& this hunger, this wringing

of guts & dry tongue. What the fuck was a tomorrow? Back then today
was *3 for 20, 2 for 10, red cap blue cap let's make a deal!*
I need four chicken wings & pork fried rice—shit is real!

★

I know what you're thinking—Groundhog Day is a comedy
& this poem sounds like your favorite rapper's first album.

It's true—I'm the metaphorical caterpillar cocooned & emerged
a butterfly & it's beautiful to flutter in sunshine—everyone
pimping. My predators are wasps, snakes, lizards & parasitic flies.

★

The joke is Bill Murray reliving the same day again & again.

Good people, we ain't no joke, we are sharing the same stories,
songs & poems over a span of decades—same but different

again & again, rewind—har har hardy har har. Are you not entertained?
I should've been an exquisite corpse.

My yesterdays are my today—every day—I can't trust tomorrow.

Praise Poem: Nazim Hikmet
—*after Jan Heller Levi*

For your olive trees,
your bullets & tanks
& prison bars—the letters
the long & heartbreaking
letters, for your many deaths
on paper & for your elegies
mourning each one, for
your friends, for Mustafa,
for the strangest creature
on earth, for your pot of honey
& for your wife—ever absent,
ever present, for your hymns
& your exile, one holding space
for the other, & for your honey
pot red as fire! & for your bees.

Variation on a theme by Rumi

Start with patience—with longing.
O longing—thorny vine growing
from the dirt of my mind—I begin again
in a pin prick, a trickle tightly running
down your body's slender pockets, each
one enough for my mouth, my fingertips
to catch on, to wait patiently within.
O to love by longing—patiently—forming
stars in the roof of my mouth, kissing
starry cinders into a wine we devour
from cupped hands—beloved, be lunatic
be savage, be a wink & a grin sent across
an ocean, be thirst, the hands holding
my face & laughing—start with patience
believe me, O longing, believe in me
the way starving *forget-me-nots* believe
in sun & water & be the question beloved
be question & the patience of searching,
never finding answers—only longing after them.

Elegy for Gabo
—*for Gabriel Garcia Marquez*

Did you wear the black shoes,
the patent leather ones?

The streets are clean
where you are going, or
so they say.

Gabo, take a little detour
down this fine powder road,
to the wooden shack
where the beers are colder
than cruelty.

All the tables & chairs are dressed
in cheesecloth, the lovers,

sex workers, & soldiers you fathered
wait to smell your cologne one last time.

Please come for the day,
I am roasting a pig in a matchbox,
the village tailor is making
a suit for you—out of palm leaves.
The colonel organized a parade,

we are naming the town after you
follow me down the road.

It is here, just the way you wrote it,
vamos Gabo, come back to us.

Elegy for all of it

Sometimes, if I catch a white person staring
at me, as I hop in my car, I imagine

them calculating whether or not I need reparations.
I mean, they don't know I'm Afro-Latino.

To white racists black is black, which is true but not
in the way they think it's true.

★

I was almost done eating my beef & broccoli
when a white woman strolled into Chow's Wok
& ordered:

> *A pint of plain white rice please, just white rice.*

I heard the owner ask, *Nothing else?*

She repeated *Just plain white rice please.*

A short standoff ensued, very short,

> *Should I take your money or spit in your face* short.

The proprietor shouted the order to the kitchen.
Shortly, the white rice & the money changed hands.

★

My daughter Lily brought home a Black History Month project.
I love baseball so she chose Jackie Robinson.

She read me the short story she was given about Jackie Robinson's life:

> *Jackie Robinson was the first black man to play in the major leagues.*
> *In order to play in the majors Jackie had to control his anger.*

Pause. I flip ahead, I flip back to the cover, I flip
through the assignment instructions, but there is no
explanation as to why Jackie Robinson had to control his anger.

No racist white ball players.
No racist white fans in the stadium.
No segregation in baseball.
No racism.

Institutions will erase racism from history
but be racist every single day.

★

The Monday after Tamir Rice's murder
many white people I knew went on with their lives,

their social media feeds a mix of ironic humor
& smiling faces & anything but black lives mattering.

I hit like on some of them, waited
a few minutes & hit unlike & let that hang in the air.

Hopefully, they struggled with what that meant.
The day we learned of Alton Sterling's murder I ate

a long lunch with a white friend, maybe two hours,
& they never brought it up. The next day Philando Castile

was murdered, & they never brought it up.
It went on like this for a while. I counted.

Dear Reader, I've heard white people say,
I don't know. I didn't want to get too heavy.

Laugh out loud. At these times I think

of *[Insert white celebrity getting rich off black culture].*

Patron saint of white silence.

Dear White Reader, we're being slaughtered *catch as catch can.*

By all means, go back to your Daily Dose of Internet video.

★

We watch men & women level buildings, super-heroes—we call them,
watch them explode planets & kill millions, we watch for entertainment
—it tastes good to us.

★

Walking around Times Square one day
a Buddhist grabbed my wrist & tied
a bracelet to it.

He offered me countless blessings. He said
the bracelet would protect me & he gave
me a little rolled piece of parchment for good
fortune.

I asked, *What's the catch?*

You see, we're building a temple. He replied.
& we'd like a donation of ten or twenty dollars.

I honestly had no cash on me. I apologized.
He quickly untied the bracelet, took back his parchment
& left. That's capitalism.

★

In "Poem for Yusef Hawkins," Felipe Luciano writes:

> *When black people march back to the sea,*
> *they're taking America with them.*
> *And no one will be able to stop them.*

Amen.

★

In the drawing, "The Execution of French Soldiers,"
Haitian revolutionaries are hanging the titular soldiers

well into the background for miles & even up
into the mountains. The drawing is black & white

but the sky was certainly Caribbean blue & the sun
had to be cooking that wool & silk uniform. Sweat
& rope burning the neck flesh.

If you look closely you can see a kind of frenzy
on the Haitian's faces. What a spectacular way

to end your oppression, to change places with the
lash-master who just the week before, probably,

beat the blood from your skin. Spectacular.

★

Eric Garner Michael Brown Tamir Rice

Walter Scott Alton Sterling Philando Castile

Stephon Clark Breonna Taylor George Floyd

Amadou Diallo Kenneth Chamberlain

Jonathan Ferrell John Crawford III Jordan Edwards

Botham Jean Atatiana Jefferson Eleanor Bumpers

Alberta Spruill Sandra Bland Tony McDade

Aiyana Stanley-Jones Kathryn Johnston

Deborah Danner Kalief Browder Trayvon Martin

Edmond Perry Jose Garcia Henry Dumas

Michael Stewart Randolph Evans Jordan Davis

Rayshard Brooks Yusef Hawkins Oscar Grant

Freddie Gray Sam Dubose Terence Crutcher

Jamar Clark Jeremy McDole William Chapman II

Eric Harris Akai Gurley Carlos Ingram Lopez

Sean Monterrosa Jose Soto Israel Hernandez-Llach

Elijah McClain Magdiel Sanchez Daniel Harris

Every year, of every decade, there is a list. Remember that.

The Cost

   —for Aracelis Girmay

1.

My black folk believe we fell from grace,
we fell walking the path & bad
language, philosophy, or faith brought the Europeans
upon us. We paid a price we didn't
decide. Now, we know the cost.

One night, singing in my sleep I had a dream
of a steady rocking like a metronome.
In the dream—I felt a rough brown hand
on my head & heard him sigh, *I am Esteban,* he said.

I opened my mouth & candies fell out.
An offering, cried Esteban, *we begin!*
Half-naked in a filthy loincloth I stood on a wooden
deck, moldy mast, Portuguese flag stitched in sail,
entire ship in flames & sailing along.
Esteban waved, *Come, mulato, see the first shore.*

Tree-dressed mountains, cotton clouds & blue skies,
this island & so many like it—clear waters, pink sands.
Our people dancing & drinking, dressed like lords,
grinding each other to calypso, bachata, soca.

Our flags: red & blue, black & red, yellow & green.

Closer, sand choking on beer & tequila bottles.
The bloody shackled feet of carnival dancers.
Resorts—shining pools of water in the hills,
a white man posed on a flat green patch, I thought
he waved at us, he was testing the wind, swung
his golf club, wind pressed tee shirt over
his belly—ALL INCLUSIVE in bold black letters.

Esteban laughed a bitter laugh.
The waters began to rise & rise.
Hurricanes spun—a seascape, the carnival
never stopped, costumes & all the storm dragged
island folk off land. The resorts & white men golfing
blew bubbles & sank to the depths without a sound.
The water so clear you'd see Middle Passage dead
at the bottom.

What are my brothers & sisters thinking
as they dance? After all the declarations
of independence, decades pretending
white government white wigs & all?

The European colonies exist
unchanged in our minds.

Esteban grabbed me by the neck & asked:

What do you see in the water?

2.

You are sixteen & at a pool party. The girls are pretty. The party is a Latino party, but you know the drill. Your own family warns you against dating black people. Yet here you are, the only black person at the party. Latino, yes (whatever that means), but black. As the time to enter the pool approaches, gradually, less & less "friends" engage you. You feel like a guest that's not being asked to leave, but you feel like a guest that's no longer wanted. The other kids start getting into the pool. No one is inviting you. No one is acknowledging you. Foolishly, you start speaking to people in Spanish. You are trying to prove something. No one is listening. You are ashamed of your desperation. Deep inside you—waters are crashing loudly. You leave the party & nobody notices. A few days later, at school, nobody asks you how you liked the party. They talk about it as if you weren't even there. As if you hadn't been invited. Later, you'll learn about segregation & pools. The one drop rule. The one black toe in the water rule. Across *todas Las Américas.* You learn that DNA is genetic memory—just like water. You learn we paid a price we didn't decide. Now, we know the cost.

3.

My son asks why he's not brown like me.

I have the other
talk with him, about passing
& not being able to pass
& don't you even think about passing.

Memory takes the moment—I'm running
in the rain with friends
the rain stops against my hair, sits
like cold wax on a wooden table.
My afro is not grass laying under water's weight.

Your hair's not soft like mine. You can't do this.

The hand a buffing pad—makes a shine,
a lacquered lawn I want to torch.
        So, I slap my friend, in the name
of that narrative:

white is good, black is bad
good hair, bad hair.
        You shall not pass.

& I tell my son that…

4.

I want(ed) to wake up—

Esteban gave me a bottle of rum.
Colonizers gave us these islands,
little fiefdoms of diaspora, a trap.

Colonizers really loved the weather, but in the end
we became intolerable, now
they rule us with banks.

How long to make slaves into a kingdom again?
Little islands—diaspora of Babel,
& the more I drank the more Esteban cried
& his tongue crawled out of his mouth—a great snake.

Give me the bottle.
Donne moi la bouteille.
Dame la botella.
Geef me de fles.

We paid a price we didn't decide.
Now, we know the cost.

Mixtape for City Kids from Dysfunctional but Happy Families, Kids Like Me *(Bonus Cut)*

You seen what I see too. A smile that ain't a smile but teeth
flying against our necks. I feel like it's just me look, I feel
like I can't breathe look, I feel like I can't sleep look, I feel
heartless, often off this feelin' of fallin', of fallin' apart
with darkest hours, lost it. I've become accustomed
to the way the ground opens up & envelops me. They require
a song of me less to celebrate my captivity than to justify
their own. But still I rise. I rise I rise I rise. Stern firm & young
with a laidback tongue the aim is to succeed & achieve...
I come from a people who remember such things who tell
stories inside the stories we are told. And, so do you.
And that's word, word to everything I love.

Elegy for Tito

There was no nightmare
only the shakes, chills, & cold sweat
a teasing pain in my kidneys
extra blankets weren't enough
neither socks nor sweaters—
I rose from bed in the morning
terrified of death & dying
& of being missed by my children.
I drove to work in self-absorbed
dread & I saw you in the parking lot.
You called out *Profésor!* in a Spanish
that praises, loves, & admires all at once.
We walked through the door together
& I made small talk—a crime really
the words wafted up like lit ash then blinked out.
You passed through another door
& I watched you on that other path
& wondered, *why would he go that way?*
Your body & the curls on your head shrinking
& I imagined you walking to the library
but my own life rushed in—a wave
urging me to keep swimming to breathe
& I forgot you & my macabre mood
& then   you died in the bathroom.
How many ways can a death be foretold
& why don't we listen when voices whisper
from the opaque lands that terrify
& wait beyond the silken veil?
Let those who have ears to hear—hear.
Tito, you might not believe I believe this,
but you are flying across all the starry nights.

Testament for the Crossover Dribble that Rocked the World
(March 12th, 1997)

1.

If Phil Jackson had known calling
Michael Jordan's name to guard
AI coming off a screen screamed
panic—then he would've invested
all his money since in a time-machine,
so he could go back to that moment
& shut his mouth.

2.

If young Allen Iverson dreamed of one day meeting
Michael Jordan after watching every game he played,
after pretending to be him, after telling everyone
he loved Michael Jordan, & how he was gonna be
Like Mike, then you can imagine his surprise
when during the 1997 All-Star Weekend, he walked
up to Michael Jordan for the first time & said hello,
& Michael Jordan replied *Wassup, you little bitch*.

3.

If 16 wins & 45 losses means you suck, if 54 wins
& 8 losses means damn near perfection, if the game
itself means nothing because their records are farther
apart than Mars & Pluto, if Allen Iverson hadn't sharpened
that crossover all over America playing AAU, playing
on faded courts & rims with no nets, playing championship
games in front of his mirror, while lying in his bed
every night, then why did the world jump
when Phil Jackson shouted *Michael!* then why when
Michael reached on the first crossover—did *Oh shit* slide
outta my mouth like that good *pollo* grease?

4.

If *a one, two, a one two* sets it off, if one—two a.k.a.
a two piece can be lights out for a glass chin, if one
two is a heartbeat, the blink of an eye, the sound
of wind rushing towards you as the guillotine drops,
then you missed it & had to wait for the replay,
then Michael's hand out there in the cold not once
but twice is proof kings do bleed when you cut them,
then Allen Iverson said *Who's the bitch now.* He did not ask.
One, two, one—right, left, right, jumper, swoosh, *goodnight.*

Poem for the Skateboard Collecting Dust in My Side-room

It's not so much my daughter shouting
Daddy you'll break your hip & I'll laugh
that I miss, although it kept me honest.
I miss the freedom—cruising on fat rubber
tires, a long wide board that can hold my
height & weight, & have you ever taken
a downhill, a 20-degree slope—blood
headbanging in your veins, & damnit
if it isn't like riding a hog on the highway
or surfing a board when the swell is firing,
to which I admit I've never done either, but
I am riding earth's rotation—I'm too old
for Ollie's or 360 double heel flips but baby
I can cruise up & down a block, a skate park,
my driveway—I can put off the entropy
of my organism with the open doors of my
heart & mind & my feet on the board—down
hill baby, downhill.

Landscape with Postcards from Lynne
for Lynne McEniry

& don't think it didn't cross my mind
that you have the magic ability to mete out
your heart into thin 4x6 heralds of love.
& that your postcards are also schooners
carrying us over the horizon onto an idyll
bursting with jugs of cheap wine and fine cheeses,
of gardens full of roses that smell like women
who've been dancing all night in red dresses.
The sweet scent of perfume & flesh amidst
maple trees dripping Basil Hayden sap & yes,
puppies, fucking adorable puppies everywhere.
& over each hill a beach & a salty sea full
of whales & sharks & not too far from there
a bookstore with Gerald Stern in it, just shopping & laying low
& tucked in between an outcropping of holly
a small cabin & inside it a living room lined with books.
& as we walk in, each poet with a post card in hand
a true hug from you & we know we are right again.
We dance as it rains postcards from the ceiling
& every two hours time moves backward & we gain an hour.
Please don't laugh, don't cry, you know all this is true
it has happened before & it will happen again,
& it will taste like baby apples from a small tree
where deer come & eat in the quiet morning dew.

Zuihitsu for the Day's Ashes

The sun is honey—drizzled atop my lawn,
my shed, & this weapon I hold in my hands.

Little girls really do sing, & dance all day
& after, the silence is overwhelming.

A dog is happiest with a toy in its teeth,
& if you throw it, good lord.

Lying here on the sofa—under a blanket,
it's easy to forget the world is ending.

When I'm old I hope I don't get Alzheimer's.
It's like being a photograph in your loved one's
hands—& they keep staring at it & you can't say
anything back to them.

Birds singing in the trees remind me how
discontented I am & the clouds in the sky, how small.

I've been listening to the wind lately, I know
it speaks to trees & small animals, but not to me.

Grief is an excellent companion, it never
says no to a drink, or to a second or third,
best not to let it in every night, maybe just Saturday.

I keep telling people I love them—I mean
I do, maybe I'm afraid too, I'll stop here.

Bismillāhi rahmāni rahīm—All gratitude & reverence to the almighty God, The Most Gracious, the Most Merciful.

Thank you to my publishers and reviewers, thank you for taking a chance. Thank you, dear reader, for riding with me and my poetry. Stick around beloved, more to come. "Life if a beautiful struggle." What a lucky life. Thank you. Mad love.

—Roberto Carlos Garcia

Notes

The introduction contains data and statistics from the National Institution on Aging and the Alzheimer's Association websites:

https://www.nia.nih.gov/news/studies-explore-alzheimers-risk-factors-biomarkers-latinos#:~:text=Overall%2C%2013%20percent%20of%20U.S.,Hispanic%20whites%2C%20the%20CDC%20estimates

https://www.alz.org/help-support/resources/black-americans-and-alzheimers

black /Maybe: An Afro Lyric

Sources

"Home [An Irrevocable Condition]"

Criss, Anthony, and Vincent Brown. *Uptown Anthem.* Naughty by Nature. DJ Kay Gee, 1991. Vinyl recording.

Rukeyser, Muriel. "The Poem as Mask" *Muriel Rukeyser: Selected Poems.* Ed. Adrienne Cecile. Rich. New York: Library of America, 2004. N. pag. Print.

Carter, Sean. By Kanye West, M. Price, and D. Walsh. Heart of the City (Ain't No Love). Jay-Z. Kanye West, 2001. Vinyl recording.

Def, Mos. Hip Hop. Mos Def. Diamond D, Mos Def, 1999. Vinyl recording.

"black Maybe"

Altman, Susan. "Haiti, Republic of." Encyclopedia of African-American Heritage. New York: Facts On File, 2000. History Research Center. Web. 2 Aug. 2015.

Baldwin, James. "Encounter on the Seine: Black Meets Brown." The Price of the Ticket: Collected Nonfiction, 1948-1985. New York: St Martin's, 1985. 35-39. Print.

Foley, Elise. "Deportation Separated Thousands Of U.S.-Born Children From Parents In 2013." The Huffington Post. TheHuffingtonPost.com, 25 June 2014. Web. 12 July 2015.

Perdomo, Willie. "Nigger-Reecan Blues." Where a Nickel Costs a Dime. New York: W.W. Norton, 1996. 19-21. Print.

Rankine, Claudia. "II." Citizen: An American Lyric. Minneapolis: Graywolf, 2014. 23-24. Print.

"The Global African - Hostility in the D.R., Verizon, Football." YouTube. Bill Fletcher Jr., 29 June 2015. Web. 12 July 2015.

Resources

Thomas, Piri. *Down These Mean Streets.* New York: Vintage, NY. Print.

Quiñonez, Ernesto. *Bodega Dreams.* New York: Vintage Contemporaries, 2000. Print.

Baraka, Amiri. *Tales of the out & the Gone.* New York: Akashic, 2007. Print.

Baraka, Amiri. *Preface to a Twenty Volume Suicide Note ....* New York: Totem, 1961. Print.

Baldwin, James. *Notes of a Native Son.* London: Michael Joseph, 1964. Print.

Piñero, Miguel. *La Bodega Sold Dreams.* Houston, TX: Arte Público, 1980. Print.

Reiter, Bernd, and Eison Simmons, Kimberly. *Afro-descendants, Identity, and the Struggle for Development in the Americas.* East Lansing: Michigan State UP, 2012. Print.

Perdomo, Willie. *Where a Nickel Costs a Dime.* New York: W.W. Norton, 1996. Print.

Perdomo, Willie. *Smoking Lovely.* New York, NY: Rattapallax, 2003. Print.

Ellis, Thomas Sayers. *Skin, Inc.*: Identity Repair Poems. Minneapolis, MN: Graywolf, 2010. Print.

Rankine, Claudia. *Citizen: An American Lyric.* Minnesota: Graywolf, 2014. Print.

Candelario, Ginetta E. B. *Black Behind the Ears: Dominican Racial Identity from Museums to Beauty Shops.* Durham: Duke University Press, 2007. Print.

[Elegies]

"Mixtape for City Kids from Dysfunctional but Happy Families, Kids Like Me" is a form I invented called a "mixtape." A mixtape resembles a cento in that it is composed of lines borrowed from other poets, but different because it includes lines from fiction, non-fiction, rap lyrics, & other forms of literature. A "mixtape" can be between 50 & 100 lines long & should have at least ten original lines written by the poet. The poem must also have a turn every 5 to 10 lines or so. The poets & writers in order of appearance are:

Reginald Dwayne Betts, Gil Scott Heron, Willie Perdomo, Aracelis Girmay, Jay-Z, John Murillo, Larry Levis, Rumi, & Aracelis Girmay.

(B-side) Natalie Diaz, Raquel Salas Rivera, Ross Gay, Denice Frohman, Patrick Rosal, Ta-Nehisi Coates, & James Baldwin.

(Bonus cut) Amiri Baracka, Kendrick Lamar, Eazy E, Amiri Baraka, James Baldwin, Maya Angelou, Q-Tip of Tribe Called Quest, Roger Bonair-Agard, & Willie Perdomo.

"Cento for a Mood" is a cento. The poets in order of appearance are:

Gerald Stern, Khaled Mattawa, Patricia Smith, Reza Baraheni, Gwendolyn Brooks, Samih Al-Qasim, Liu Xiaobo, & Rita Dove.

In the poem "Anton Corbin's Photo of Miles Davis" the photo was recreated by Massimo Galarza using charcoal & pencil.

"Elegy in which math proves the dead are better off without us" contains lines from *The Order of Time* by Carlo Rovelli.

Acknowledgements

Melancolía

Barrelhouse: "A riot in images"

Lunch Ticket: "What can I tell you"

Olentangy Review: A version of "Name it"

pluck! The Journal of Affrilachion Arts & Culture: "Duplicity"

Public Pool: "No currency" and "Savior complex"

The Stillwater Review: "Belief System" and "Reading Rorschach Cards"

Tuesday: An Art Project: "If my name was Yusef Aziz"

Word Peace: A version of "I cannot write anything"

5 AM: "Ars Poetica"

black /Maybe: An Afro Lyric

5 AM Magazine: "Ars Poetica" and "Burn"

Poets/Artists Magazine: "Mamá Ana's Apartment in Washington Heights" and "Art imitating death"

Connotation Press: An Online Artifact: a version of "Back to School" and "Poem for Uncle Jaime"

Atticus Review: "Coward"

Adanna Literary Journal: a version of "The dead send dreams"

The Acentos Review: "The angry Black man," "Casta," and "Identity repair poem"

Gawker: A version of "black Maybe" titled "Hiding black behind the ears: On Dominicans, blackness, & Haiti"

Seven Scribes: A version of "Home [An Irrevocable Condition]"
The title of this manuscript is inspired by the title of the song "U, Black Maybe" written and performed by the artist Common on his album *Finding Forever*.

[Elegies]

Academy of American Poets Poem-A-Day: "This moment / Right now"

Atticus Review: "Elegy for Gabo"

Best American Poetry Blog: "Mixtape for City Kids from Dysfunctional but Happy Families, Kids Like Me"

Luna Luna: "Elegy in Which I Rename A City For You" & "Elegy in Which We Are Quantum Theory"

Moonstone Arts Center: Remembering Amiri Baraka on His 85th Birthday: An Anthology: "Note to AB"

Plátano Poets Café: "Elegy in which I dream of us under fruit trees"

Part one of "A Tempest" was published in Haymarket Books' anthology *BreakBeat Poets Vol 4: LatiNext* and as part of a folio from the anthology in the March issue of *Poetry Magazine.*

Soul Sister Revue Anthology: "Elegy in the Key of Life"

Terra Preta Review: "Elegy in which grief sends me," "Elegy in which is hidden an ode to your beehive updo," & "Elegy in which 'Happy' by Pharrell sends me spiraling"

Those People: "Ten Minutes of Terror"

Printed in the USA
CPSIA information can be obtained
at www.ICGtesting.com
LVHW081540071023
760217LV00069B/1755